ON HUMANISTIC EDUCATION

Giambattista Vico

ON HUMANISTIC EDUCATION
(SIX INAUGURAL ORATIONS, 1699–1707)

FROM THE DEFINITIVE LATIN TEXT,
INTRODUCTION, AND NOTES
OF GIAN GALEAZZO VISCONTI

༺⚜༻

Translated by
Giorgio A. Pinton and Arthur W. Shippee

with an Introduction by
Donald Phillip Verene

Cornell University Press
Ithaca and London

Authorization to base the English translation on the Latin text edited and annotated by Gian Galeazzo Visconti, *Le Orazioni Inaugurali, I–VI* (Bologna: Il Mulino, 1982), volume 1 of *Opere di Giambattista Vico* commissioned by the Centro di Studi Vichiani, has been granted by the director of the Centro di Studi Vichiani, Naples, Italy.

The summaries of the Orations are reprinted from *The Autobiography of Giambattista Vico,* translated by Max Harold Fisch and Thomas Goddard Bergin, copyright © 1944 by Cornell University and used by permission of the publisher, Cornell University Press.

First published 1993 by Cornell University Press.

International Standard Book Number 0-8014-2838-6 (cloth)
International Standard Book Number 0-8014-8087-6 (paper)
Library of Congress Catalog Card Number 92-56787

Printed in the United States of America

Librarians: Library of Congress cataloging information appears on the last page of the book.

♾ The paper in this book meets the minimum requirements of the American National Standard for Information Sciences—Permanence of Paper for Printed Library Materials, ANSI Z39.48-1984.

Contents

꿀꾳꿀

ON HUMANISTIC EDUCATION

Introduction:
On Humanistic Education

༄

Donald Phillip Verene

I

We live in a scientific and technological world in which the quest for certainty and method has become a substitute for the search for truth. The clear idea and the unambiguous statement are the ideal of the modern thinker and of modern education. The ancient conceptions of rhetoric as a part of logic and of metaphor as essential to thought, which Aristotle said was the greatest thing to master and a sign of genius,[1] have become largely lost to us as elements of what we count as basic to human knowledge. We are inspired not by the turn of phrase, the sudden perception of a similarity in dissimilars, or the strength of memory, but by clarity and certainty, which go hand in hand and inspire our confidence in our ability to control the object of our thought. When we are able methodologically to order the contents of our experience so successfully that we can move about the world with a certainty not known to the ancients, the search for truth seems to become unnecessary.

When the self can truly possess the object it desires, certainty becomes the form of its moment of satisfaction. The methods of modern science and research allow us to accomplish this grasp of the object in thought; technology allows us to possess it in fact.

1. *Poetics* 1459a 5–9.

The modern self—that which, with Descartes, knows it exists because it thinks (and knows it can put this thought into action)—is the owner of the world. The greatest thing to be is the master of method, not the master of metaphor; for method brings with it the possibility of certainty, or near certainty, and metaphor brings only ambiguity and possibilities of meaning that perhaps can never be fully known. Truth, as opposed to certainty, has always placed the self as thinker in relation to the whole, or to the divine, as something that is beyond the reality of the self.

Hegel, in a famous statement, says, "The True is the whole."[2] Vico says in *On the Study Methods of Our Time*, "the whole is really the flower of wisdom."[3] The search for truth has classically always placed the human in relation to something beyond the reach of any method or form of self-contained, step-by-step thinking and analyzing. The self's search for truth has commonly prized *ingenium* (the perception of connections among what otherwise seem separate) over method; imagination (as the power to form true images) over abstraction and classification; and reason (as the metaphysical attempt to know fully) over ratiocination (as a process of intellectual ordering of specific content).

The modern quest for certainty transposes the ancient search for truth and the whole into the logician's conception of the whole as the set of all true propositions about the world. The search for truth—since Socrates—has been rooted in the indefinite enterprise called self-knowledge, the dictate on the Temple of Apollo at Delphi: "Know thyself," what ancients and humanists alike thought of as human wisdom, the true end of human thought and the love of it: philosophy.

The French historian Paul Hazard has said: "If only Italy had listened to Giambattista Vico, and if, as at the time of the Renaissance, it had served as a guide to Europe, would not our intellectual destiny have been different? Our eighteenth-century ancestors

2. G. W. F. Hegel, *Phenomenology of Spirit*, trans. A. V. Miller (Oxford: Oxford University Press, 1977), p. 11.
3. *On the Study Methods of Our Time*, trans. Elio Gianturco; preface by Donald Phillip Verene (1965; new ed. Ithaca: Cornell University Press, 1990), p. 77.

would not have believed that all that was clear was true; but on the contrary that 'clarity is the vice of human reason rather than its virtue,' because a clear idea is a finished idea. They would not have believed that reason was our first faculty, but on the contrary that imagination was."[4]

The ideal of modern education has listened not to Vico but to Descartes and Leibniz—to the Port Royal logic as a model of Cartesian education—which excludes education in the arts of speech, memory, and the metaphor (the poetic and rhetorical) in favor of the analytical and methodologically clear;[5] to the promotion of a *characteristica universalis*, the Leibnizian idea of an order of symbolism, in which all can be unambiguously formulated; and to the conception of human knowledge of the French encyclopaedists, the *philosophes*, for whom the model of knowledge was not self-knowledge but the specific treatment of a particular subject in a single article, bringing out its nature with clarity and wit for any intelligent reader to grasp. Each of these—the analytic chain of reasoning, the universal formulation, the encyclopaedia article as the complete treatment of a subject—is a model of an anonymous form of knowledge. Each produces a mastery of the world, but not a mastery of the self or a wisdom of its actions in the human world that was classically known as prudence (Gr. *phronēsis*, L. *prudentia*). Self-knowledge is never by nature analytic, formal, or article in nature. The Delphic instruction, its divinely inspired speech, calls out to the human for something other than such a model of human knowledge can supply.

The major theme of Vico's orations is self-knowledge, under-

---

4. Paul Hazard, *La pensée européenne au XVIIIe siècle de Montesquieu à Lessing* (Paris: Arthine Fayard, 1963), p. 43. My trans.

5. A. Arnauld and P. Nicole, *La logique ou l'art de penser: Contenant, outre les règles communes, plusieurs observations nouvelles, propres à former le jugement*, critical ed. by P. Clair and F. Girbal (Paris: Presses Universitaires de France, 1965).

The above claim concerning the dominance of this ideal of modern scientistic education does not mean that other forms of education totally disappeared in the modern age. It does not apply to classical education, which was alive and well into the first part of this century; and it does not apply to pedagogical traditions in the humanities that have resisted movements such as positivism in historical, literary, and philosophical studies.

stood in the sense Socrates spoke about it in the agora of Athens. Vico makes this the theme of the first oration, quoting the Delphic inscription: Know thyself (*Temet nosce*). A second theme is wisdom (*sapientia*), which Vico connects with the goal of self-knowledge. He says to the students to whom the oration is addressed: "You are born for wisdom" (par. 4). Vico joins the dictum of the Temple of Apollo, which came to be identified as the general Socratic ideal, with the Aristotelian dictum that all humans by nature desire to know. The desire to know is a natural inclination, the highest form of which is to know one's own human "spirit" (*animus*). The highest form of knowledge is for the human knower to know what makes the human, human. What is the nature and meaning of our humanity? Vico says he takes from Cicero this emphasis that self-knowledge means to know one's own *animus*. Behind this is also the dictum, which Cicero makes much of, that wisdom is "a knowledge of things human and divine."[6] Humans must seek not simply a self-contained wisdom, but one predicated on an understanding of the difference between what is human and what is divine.

Vico mentions that the dictum "Know thyself" was attributed to Pythagoras, among other ancients, and by selecting Pythagoras from among the seven sages he may intend the reader to have in mind an echo of the traditional account of the origin of the name and nature of philosophy, the fullest report of which comes from Cicero, who relates an episode originally reported by Heraclides of Pontus, in which Pythagoras was made to explain philosophy to Leon, the tyrant of Phlius. Leon asked Pythagoras whether he possessed any particular skill or wisdom. Pythagoras replied with a play on *sophia*, describing himself as a *philosophos*—not wise, but a "lover of wisdom."[7]

In this way Pythagoras separated himself from any claim to possess the superhuman powers of the gods, or even of the wise

---

6. See Cicero, *Tusc.* IV.26.57 and *De off.* II.2.5. Seneca, *Letters to Lucilius* 89.5, states that "wisdom is knowledge of things human and divine"; this was taken up later by Renaissance thinkers, and it became a commonplace definition of wisdom. See *Study Methods*, pp. 49–50.

7. Cicero, *Tusc.* V.3.7ff. See the translation and commentary in H. B. Gottschalk, *Heraclides of Pontus* (Oxford: Clarendon Press, 1980), pp. 23–36.

figures of the heroic age such as Ulysses or Nestor. Pythagoras further separated himself from other parts of the human community by comparing the philosopher to a particular type of person attending the great games at Olympia, saying that some go to the games to compete with their bodies for fame and honor; others go for the possibilities of profit and gain in the activities of buying and selling that take place there; and some go only to watch and see what is happening, wishing neither applause nor profit. These pure spectators are like those who in life live not for fame or profit but for the possibility of contemplating the universe. These are the philosophers.

Although Vico's references in these orations and elsewhere are most often to classical authors and to Renaissance humanist texts, he, like Saint Augustine, attempts to merge pagan wisdom with Christian doctrine. Like Saint Augustine (whom Vico calls, in another place, "my particular protector"),[8] Vico quotes pagan classical authors while endorsing the ends of Christian religion. Vico can claim, with Socrates,[9] that wisdom itself "is the property of God," that is, Vico is careful not to claim that his conception of wisdom includes what can be known only by the God of the Christian religion. With the Renaissance humanists and with Cicero, however, he advocates the possibility of the attainment of a human wisdom. Vico is, of course, not unique in claiming the "Christian relevance" of pagan ideas, which was fundamental to humanism from Petrarch on.

The complexity of Vico's relationship to religion is a problem in itself, and one that cannot be pursued here.[10] Throughout these orations Vico often relies on pagan authors and yet insists on the relevance of their ideas to Christian ends. We would not expect him to do otherwise, in that these orations are an official duty of his university position, the University of Naples is an institution of

---

8. *Opere di G. B. Vico*, ed. F. Nicolini (8 vols. in 11) (Bari: Laterza, 1911–41), 5:377.

9. *Apology* 23a. But at 20d-e Socrates does say that he may be considered wise in human things.

10. See my comments on Vico and religion in *The New Art of Autobiography: An Essay on the "Life of Giambattista Vico Written by Himself"* (Oxford: Clarendon Press, 1991), pp. 41–44 and 190.

the state, and Catholicism is the religion of Naples. Max Fisch has pointed out that it is not possible to understand Vico's thought without knowing that the Inquisition operated in Naples throughout his lifetime.[11] Only six years before Vico's first oration, three of his friends had been imprisoned by the Inquisition, an event that made a strong impression on him.

Throughout his career Vico was professor of rhetoric at the University of Naples. His title was "Royal Professor of Eloquence" (specifically, Latin eloquence). But the position itself, in its prestige and remuneration, was not nearly so grand as the title. He was an expert on Latin authors and classical learning in general, and he was imbued with the humanist ideal of education. He claimed to know Latin as well as his own language—both to read and to write it with ease. The idea of education that he advocates in these orations (and throughout his entire career) might best be summed up in relation to the intersection of three terms—*sapientia, eloquentia,* and *prudentia.*

Sapientia, or human wisdom, for Vico refers to the achievement of self-knowledge. Self-knowledge does not refer to some form of psychological introspection or to any form of introspection at all. It means, for Vico, that the student should study the entire curriculum of thought. The student should take the whole of human knowledge as his province. The fields of human knowledge form a cycle that should be gone through completely. And as is evident from his sixth oration, this cycle is to be approached and studied in a particular order, with certain studies coming first and serving as background for others. Behind Vico's thinking here is certainly the scheme of the seven liberal arts of the Trivium (grammar, rhetoric, and logic) and Quadrivium (arithmetic, music, geometry, and astronomy) and the *Studia humanitatis,* which the humanists created by excluding logic from the Trivium and adding history, Greek, moral philosophy, and poetry to grammar and rhetoric.

Also in Vico's mind is the general quarrel between the ancients and the moderns—the rise of the modern sciences based on exper-

---

11. Max Harold Fisch, Introduction to *The Autobiography of Giambattista Vico,* trans. M. H. Fisch and Thomas Goddard Bergin (1944; rpt. Ithaca: Cornell University Press, 1983), p. 34.

iment and indicative ways of thinking, as opposed to the arts of composition, speech, and memory: the arts necessary for the conduct of civil affairs, in which the ancients excelled. The attempt to find a balance in education and thought between the empirical and scientific specialist methods of knowledge in the sciences and the arts of poetry, rhetoric, and jurisprudence of classical thought is the subject of Vico's *On the Study Methods of Our Time*, which, although originally drafted as an oration, became a small book in itself, published during his lifetime.[12]

Eloquentia, or eloquence, is understood by Vico as different from simply elegant or ornate forms of statement. Eloquence, in the way Vico most often thinks of it, does not refer to the beauty of the words that a writer or speaker may use. Eloquence does not refer to the fine turns of phrase that may be used, although these are of considerable importance. It refers instead to the ability to speak about the whole of the subject. Eloquence is the quality a speech needs to be complete, to encompass all the dimensions of a subject, to connect up its smallest details and its largest dimensions and perspectives, to make a beginning and to speak through to an end that takes each listener through all the relevant aspects of the subject, including digressions, but brings the listener always back to the point and brings the whole of the topic well into view. Vico, following Cicero, holds that "eloquence is wisdom put into language."[13]

Vico concludes his autobiography with remarks on how he attempted to conduct his own teaching, saying that he always endeavored to be wisdom speaking *(sapienza che parla).*[14] If the object of wisdom is the whole of a subject, then the object of eloquence is to speak in a manner that will present the nature of this whole in words. *Res* and *verbum,* thing and word, are to be joined in the act of philosophical speech. The love of wisdom,

---

12. See above, n. 3; and Joseph M. Levine, "Vico and the Ancients and Moderns," *Journal of the History of Ideas* 52 (1991): 55–79.
13. Cicero, *De part. orat.* 23.79. The above conception of "eloquence" also applies to "elegance" in the history of rhetoric in figures such as Valla and generally in the eighteenth century. The connotation of "elegance" as vacant ornateness is a later usage.
14. *Autobiography,* p. 199.

which is to be the goal of the student, must be love of the word as the medium of wisdom—or the love of eloquence. It is typical of Vico to take a rhetorical theme in the earlier humanist tradition and transform it into a philosophical principle.

Prudentia (prudence) is the Latin cognate for the Greek *phronēsis* or practical wisdom. *Sapientia* and *eloquentia* are themes that run throughout these first six orations. *Prudentia* is an especially strong theme in the sixth oration. *Prudentia* shares its meaning with *providentia*—the notion of providence, which is divine wisdom, the wisdom that can be found when the action of God in the world is understood—and with the notion of providential action in human affairs undertaken in politics or in individual human relations.

In his later work on universal law and in the *Study Methods*, Vico makes clear that he subscribes to the opening claim of the Roman *Digest*, the basis of all Western law and the source to which, in many ways, we can trace all forms of proper human conduct in Western society: that jurisprudence is philosophy.[15] Jurisprudence is prudence guided by law or right (*ius*), the proper conduct of communal life, just as prudence or practical wisdom is what is required by any individual in order to have wisdom in particular civil affairs. The love of wisdom, or philosophy, is in essence the love of prudent or wise conduct in the *polis*, the civil world. Vico makes clear that the effect of the achievement of self-knowledge, of proper education and study, is the ability to conduct oneself in accord with one's own human nature, which is the divine element in human beings. As the divine wisdom is a kind of prudence or providence in the world in general, so the realization of true education in the individual will result in a prudence of actions and affairs.

In the fifth oration Vico considers this idea of the effect of proper study and cultivation of knowledge in relation to the achievement of power in commonwealths. He claims that the states that have most cultivated knowledge in their body politic have attained the most power. Vico does not connect human education with the search for purely theoretical knowledge. Self-

---

15. See *New Art of Autobiography*, pp. 137–47.

knowledge is always moral in the sense of being practical wisdom, a wisdom that directs the human being in life. He quotes here, and elsewhere, Horace's remark (also to be found in Cicero) that Socrates brought moral philosophy down from the heavens.[16] The knowledge of things human and divine is self-knowledge, and all self-knowledge has as its goal a knowledge of how to live.

The knowledge of how to live, that is, the knowledge of proper human action, requires that the person grasp the whole of any situation of any subject that is important to him and that this whole be put into words so it can be objectified and understood. The vision that *prudentia* introduces in human affairs requires the individual to have *sapientia,* a wisdom of the whole, and to be able for himself and for others to put this whole into words, to have *eloquentia.* The foresight required for prudence requires that the totality of a situation be understood and expressed completely and articulately.

Sapientia, eloquentia, and *prudentia* are three aspects of a total process of the human mind and spirit that is to be the true aim of humanistic education. This is a rhetorical conception of human knowledge tied to how we make sense together as language-using animals. It stands in opposition to what Vico saw as a Cartesian conception of human education, which would advocate the reduction of all thought and language to a single method of right reasoning, such that anything that was not subject to placement within the steps of this method was excluded from human knowledge, or at least discounted as illusion or as basically unimportant. Vico associates truth with life, and there is no method for life or the discovery of its means, its right conduct, and so on. As Vico holds in *On the Most Ancient Wisdom of the Italians,* anyone who would attempt to live a life or make a speech by the geometric method engages in a form of rational madness.[17]

Vico's ideal of humanistic education, which he presents for the

16. Horace, *Epistola ad Pisones (Ars Poetica),* 309–11. Vico wrote, in his "L'epistola di Orazio ai Pisoni al lume della *Scienza nuova,*" *Opere,* 7:76, that the *New Science* was a "perpetual commentary" on Horace's verses. Cicero *Tusc.* V.4.10 and *Acad.* I.4.15 ff.

17. *On the Most Ancient Wisdom of the Italians Unearthed from the Origins of the Latin Language,* trans. L. M. Palmer (Ithaca: Cornell University Press, 1988), pp. 98–99.

first time in these orations but develops in his later writings, has generally been lost in contemporary education. These is no commonly perceived ideal of modern education, unless it is simply to attempt to organize things so as to have people move along with technology, to train the mind and socialize the spirit to a world of techniques. But since there is no goal, no *telos*, education in both the sciences and the liberal arts suffers and becomes confused. We have, as Ernst Cassirer has called it, a "Crisis in Man's Knowledge of Himself," because no dominant context is present in which to understand the human being in modern life. This results in the fragmentation of the human into as many parts as there are major directions of human thought and activity.[18] Because we have lost the sense of self-knowledge as the goal of education, education in the mathematical and behavioral sciences has suffered—as it has also in the humanities and the fields of social thought.

Without a sense of the whole such as Vico advocates, there is no purpose to the study of the sciences of nature. Vico does not directly discuss this lack, but it can be vaguely felt, and it contributes to the fact that science is often badly taught and badly done. The reaction of the humanities has been to imitate the sciences by advocating some alternative procedure, such as "interpretation," and some doctrine of the text or even some form of hermeneutics that offers a way to the mastery of letters. The tradition of "humane letters" has become confused, resulting in the inability truly to teach the subject matters of the humanities—to teach the dates of historical events, to teach by repetition the forms of verbs, to have students memorize poems and speeches as examples for life. Once the humanist ideal of self-knowledge is given up, there can be no real pursuit of moral philosophy. Ethics becomes either *meta*ethics, that is, a theoretical enterprise, or applied, that is, reduced to discussion of special problems for particular areas of society. The humanist conception of moral philosophy is lost because the notion of the prudential has been lost, along with wisdom or *sapientia*, which has been replaced by a methodological conception of human knowledge.

18. Ernst Cassirer, *An Essay on Man: An Introduction to a Philosophy of Human Culture* (New Haven: Yale University Press, 1944), chap. 1.

Language becomes impoverished because, when right reasoning requires only the clarity of method, we no longer need to use language to speak about what can barely be expressed—what is beyond language and indefinite in human experience—things human and divine. We no longer need to use language to bring out the ambiguous meanings of words and things.

Cartesian method fits *res* perfectly with *verbum* by leaving out all that is problematic in the human soul. Modern life, in Vico's view, as it is developed in his stages of ideal eternal history in his major work, the *New Science*, is an island of certainty and specific knowledge, surrounded by an ocean of uncertainty and lost wisdom. In the *New Science* he refers to this state of modern life as the "barbarism of reflection."[19] Had he known it, he might have seen this state of affairs as very like that image Kant speaks of in the first *Critique*, the island of the analytic of the understanding, surrounded by the stormy ocean and fog banks of illusion of metaphysical and dialectical thought—except that Kant sees it a blessed isle.[20]

We, as modern readers who can grasp what the loss of self-knowledge as an education and epistemic ideal means—in terms of the loss of the rhetorical conception of language and of the loss of the grounding of moral philosophy in prudence—can meet again this ideal of true humanistic education in Vico, and in particular in these orations. They are important because in them we encounter Vico beginning to make the meaning of this ideal for himself, in his own thought. He develops this, in one sense, throughout his life, because pedagogical interests always guide his thought, even in the *New Science*. It is a work for the total education of humanity.

It is not my aim here to summarize the content of each of these orations because Vico has done that himself in his account of them in his *Autobiography* (the relevant paragraphs are reproduced in the text). But some remarks here may be useful as a guide to the line of thought that he is developing in these orations, lest the reader become initially discouraged and regard what Vico is say-

19. *The New Science of Giambattista Vico*, trans. Thomas Goddard Bergin and Max Harold Fisch (Ithaca: Cornell University Press, 1988), par. 1106.
20. Kant, *Critique of Pure Reason*, B 295, A 236.

ing as simply archaic and quaint. Some of his comments are difficult to accept, for today's reader, and they may have been so even for his audience at the time. He is often preachy, lofty, moralistic, and high-minded. Such approaches and tones may turn the reader away, thinking that Vico's words are shallow. I think they are not and that the sympathetic reader must be determined to overlook some of this as typical of such a speech (a little bit like a commencement address, or possibly a convocation speech in today's university). These were orations for ceremonial occasions, but they also, to Vico's mind, were occasions in which he was determined to launch the beginnings of his philosophy. He planned to publish them as part of a book, the contents for which he wrote out.

So here we see a philosopher's position in the making, and it is done by trying to get us to recall the essential ideas of the classical and humanist tradition that was being lost, even in Vico's day—and with it the basis of humanistic education. If, for the Roman *Digest*, jurisprudence is philosophy, we could say that for Vico, pedagogy is also philosophy. That is, the basis of pedagogy must be the love of wisdom, and when anyone is properly educated in this manner, there is nothing left for philosophy to be or to teach.

Vico delivered these six orations to begin the academic year as part of his position as a professor of rhetoric. They are all dated as October 18, the Feast Day of St. Luke, between 1699 (the year Vico assumed his university position) and 1707. The inaugural of 1708, the seventh, was planned by the University of Naples as a special event, to be dedicated to the Austrian king and delivered in the presence of his viceroy, Cardinal Grimani, because in 1707 the Austrians had occupied Naples, putting an end to the previous Spanish role. This seventh oration was written by Vico as a small monograph and published the following year (*Study Methods*).

Vico has two other later orations on the nature of education and the importance of humane letters for it. The first is his university oration "On the Heroic Mind," delivered in 1732 (he had published the second version of his *New Science* in 1730).[21] The other

21. "On the Heroic Mind," trans. Elizabeth Sewell and Anthony C. Sirignano, in *Vico and Contemporary Thought*, ed. G. Tagliacozzo, M. Mooney, and D. P. Verene (Atlantic Highlands, N.J.: Humanities Press, 1979).

is his oration to the Academy of Oziosi (one of several important bodies of scholars, which, in Vico's day, held private meetings for discussion and study), "The Academies and the Relation between Eloquence and Philosophy," delivered in 1737, several years before his death.[22] It is Vico's last philosophical work. All the topics developed in these later works are broached in the first six orations.

Vico saw these six orations as a single, multifaceted argument about the tradition of humane letters and its importance for modern education, as well as about how education in such ideals could be implemented in the system of education or the curriculum. Readers will wish to follow out Vico's themes on their own, but each oration is short and so easily stated that the importance of what he is saying can be missed. Because the occasion was a speech that could be delivered in a time short enough to hold the attention of a young audience, Vico usually simply states a point but does not develop it, as he could in a work written for print. It may be useful to keep in mind some of the general argument Vico is making from one oration to the next.

2

Oration I

In many ways the most important orations are the first and the last. In the first, Vico establishes the view that self-knowledge is the goal of human education and that we must study the fields of knowledge in respect to how they make up a whole. In the last oration Vico reaffirms the principle of studying the entire universe or cycle of liberal arts and sciences and presents the correct order in which these studies should be undertaken. Orations II through V raise questions about and bring forth the benefits of such a conception of education for the individual, society, and state. These orations in many ways concern the general theme of

22. "The Academies and the Relation between Philosophy and Eloquence," trans. D. P. Verene, in *On the Study Methods of Our Time* (1990).

prudence—what is possible in the sense of practical wisdom as a result of education in wisdom and eloquence of speech.

One of the major themes of the first oration, besides wisdom and self-knowledge, is what the Greeks knew as *paideia*. In Greek, *paideia* means a great range of things, from education to culture to tradition, and much in between. In some ways it is captured in modern language by the German term *Bildung*, or the idea of *Bildungsroman*: a literary work that relates the total education of a person and what that person becomes as a sentient, thinking human being. *Paideia* is the concept of education as a humane and humanizing process, as distinct from the simple study and mastery of subject matters in a curriculum. In that concept of subject matter, success in education is equivalent to what can be intellectually learned and mastered. This for Vico is ultimately the modern or Cartesian notion of education, the mastery of right reasoning in the sciences, the proper employment of the method of thinking Descartes outlines in the *Discourse on Method*.

Paideia as an ideal, however, is the notion of bringing the student as a whole to a level of human culture. This process is distinct from any system of education or curriculum. It is the actual process the human spirit goes through as it absorbs the various subject matters of human knowledge and develops a relation to them and to the world of language and civil affairs. This is not a process that is alternative to the intellectual mastery of subjects. It fully endorses and includes the absolute importance of straight learning, but it does not see such mastery as separate from the education of the citizen and the true achievement of humaneness. *Paideia* is in a sense circular in that the individual must go through the full course of study, the full curriculum of culture. This sense of the formation of the individual as a total course, going from beginning to end, has perhaps a resonance with Vico's later conception of the collective life of humanity. Humanity realizes itself as a world of nations, with each nation being born and running an entire course of its own self-formation in accordance with an overall divine order of Providence—the famous *corsi e ricorsi* of Vico's later *New Science* (1725, 1730, 1744).

Oration II

In the second oration Vico takes up the topic of the "fool." To the modern reader this may seem strange, even quaint. The idea of the fool (*stultus*) has long since left pedagogical theory and social theory, which is our loss. The fool appears as a theme in terms of the biblical "The fool hath said in his heart, there is no God"[23] in Saint Anselm's dialectical presentation of the importance of his ontological proof for God.[24] The fool as a human type is the theme of Sebastian Brant's work *Das Narrenschiff*, in 1494 (translated into Latin as *Stultifera navis* in 1497), by which the term "ship of fools" is introduced into every modern language and literature.[25] Brant's work contains both the Socratic conception of self-knowledge, which he sees as the corrective to falling in to foolishness, and the Christian doctrine of, through foolishness, failing to practice the virtues and falling into a life leading away from salvation. Foolishness is taken up as a Renaissance humanist ideal by Erasmus in *Praise of Folly*, in which there is a *theatrum mundi*, a theater of the world, upon the stage of which we each step to play our role in the human comedy. Erasmus wrote there the line, "the fool arrives at true prudence by addressing himself at once to the business and taking his chances."[26] Instead of trying to achieve the unachievable in pure thought, the fool simply falls to and acts.

---

23. Psa. 14:1.

24. *St. Anselm's Proslogion with a Reply on Behalf of the Fool by Gaunilo and the Author's Reply to Gaunilo*, trans. M. J. Charlesworth (Oxford: Oxford University Press, 1965).

25. Sebastian Brant, *The Ship of Fools*, trans. Edwin H. Seydel (New York: Columbia University Press, 1944). For the original text, variations, and commentary, see *Sebastian Brants Narrenschiff*, ed. Friedrich Zarncke (Hildesheim: Georg Olms, 1961).

26. Desiderius Erasmus, *The Praise of Folly*, trans. Hoyt Hopwell Hudson (Princeton: Princeton University Press, 1941), p. 36. See Walter Kaiser, *Praisers of Folly: Erasmus, Rabelais, Shakespeare* (Cambridge, Mass.: Harvard University Press, 1963); Ernesto Grassi and Maristella Lorch, *Folly and Insanity in Renaissance Literature* (Binghamton, N.Y.: Center for Medieval and Early Renaissance Studies, 1986); and William Willeford, *The Fool and His Scepter: A Study in Clowns and Jesters and Their Audience* (Evanston: Northwestern University Press, 1969).

Vico's sense of the foolish and its dangers to knowledge is more that of Brant's Christian doctrine than of Erasmus's human comedy. Vico's oration takes a very high moralistic tone—probably too moralistic, certainly so for modern readers. But his point is an old one, going back to the image of the human soul as charioteer in *Phaedrus* (246b), in which as humans we, unlike gods, drive not equally good and noble steeds but must try to manage one steed that is good and noble and one with the opposite character (see Vico's reference to Philo Judaeus in par. 9). The fool, Vico says, yields to the unrestrained inclinations of the passions and allows his conscience to be so overcome.

The tradition of the fool in relation to modern philosophy can be traced to Nicolaus Cusanus's *De docta ignorantia*, in which he advocates that the thing most useful to every scholar would be to learn that of which he is most ignorant so he can place his thought and study on the correct path. "Nothing could be more beneficial for even the most zealous searcher for knowledge than being in fact most learned in that very ignorance which is peculiarly his own."[27] Vico, in his fundamental endorsement of Socratic self-knowledge, is saying something similar, namely, that if we ignore the passions and have no way to form them and discipline them, if we remain ignorant of them and their effects, we have no hope of becoming educated in *paideia*. The problem with the rationalistic model of education, which directs the goal of study simply to the intellectual mastery of the subject matter, is that it ignores just those activities of thought that can form the passions and make them the source, not of foolishness but of meaning: poetry, rhetoric, and history. Vico does not say all of this so fully in this oration, perhaps because he is simply issuing a warning to youth about the dangers of not developing their minds and their reason as well as they develop their powers of conscience. But ultimately in Vico's thought this is the direction this theme takes, and it may be helpful to look back on it in these terms and thus not to dismiss it.

27. Nicolaus Cusanus, *Of Learned Ignorance*, trans. Fr. Germain Heron (London: Routledge & Kegan Paul, 1954), pp. 8–9.

Oration III

Vico says that the third oration is a "practical appendix" to the preceding two. He advocates in the third oration that in the republic of letters—in the world of scholarship—deceit and dishonesty, as well as the feigning of knowledge, must be deplored. Certainly in Vico's time such practices were not uncommon. Vico would himself later become a victim of them. When he engaged in the concourse for the "morning chair" of civil law he was defeated by another, whose only book was later withdrawn from the press for plagiarism. And such practices are not unknown in our own day, in which charges of falsified research emerge in the sciences and cases of plagiarism and, certainly, of empty thinking are found with some frequency in the humanities. The politics of the *polis* are always present within the politics of the academy. No one could disagree with Vico's call for honesty and the banishment of imposters from the world of knowledge. But this is really just the surface theme of his oration.

The deeper theme is stated in par. 13, where, after giving some dialogues and interchanges, he states what distinguishes the educated person from the vulgar: the "educated knows that he does not know." He concludes the oration by saying that "no one should presume to know beyond his measure." Here he is echoing Horace,[28] but his claim is philosophically of a part with the tradition of Socratic ignorance that is carried into and made the foundation of modern philosophy by Cusanus's doctrine of "learned ignorance," and it is also part of the humanist tradition going back to Petrarch's notion of "his own ignorance."

Vico emphasizes that the beginning of all wisdom is the admission of ignorance, the realization that we do not really know. This doctrine is certainly useful in science, in its investigation of nature, because it is from such an attitude of mind that hypotheses are formed. But it is against rationalistic science, which would claim, on the basis of correct reasoning from first principles, to be able to know—without actual inquiry—the nature of things. If this doc-

28. Horace *Epistles* I.7.98.

trine is highly important as a stance of mind for scientific empirical investigation, it is the absolute medium of the pursuit of self-knowledge. The human self, which is the agent that creates the world of culture and the civil world of human institutions, must always advance by admitting to itself that it does not wholly know their meaning. This is because the self as knower does not know their relation to the whole. The self in the end is a lover of wisdom but never the full possessor of wisdom.

Oration IV

The fourth and fifth orations ask the question, Of what use is a liberal education? Is it an end in itself, something that can be pursued for honor, or is it useful to society and the conduct of human affairs generally? In the final paragraph of the fourth oration (par. 10) Vico even addresses the age-old question that parents ask of educators in the liberal arts: whether their children are studying simply for the honor of receiving their degrees, or whether, from the pursuit of humane letters, they can expect to be aided in securing a living. Vico says (par. 8) that he wishes, with Socrates, to deny the distinction between *honestum* and *utile*—that is, the view that to do the honorable thing is not always the same as doing the expedient; that in the world of political action and human relations we must often look to what is effective or useful, whether or not it is of true value.

Vico wishes to argue for the value of the "liberal professions"— that they are truly useful both to the practitioner and to the state, as opposed to those professions which seek material gain, piling up properties and possessions. Vico's argument, in essence, is the one that has been written into the liberal arts education itself— that has behind it the ideal of *paideia*—that an educated citizenry is best and that education should be for the production of the whole self. Behind this is the ancient Greek and specifically the Platonic view that the aims of the citizen and the state should coincide. What is most useful is an education for life, one that equips the student with self-knowledge and a love of wisdom. The most useful education is that which teaches us how to live, and this sense of how to live presumes that we are, as Aristotle said, social animals. The human being for Vico is always essentially social. Thought and knowledge are communal, not individualistic. The ideal of humane letters presupposes the existence of the agora, the place in which to speak eloquently.

Oration V

The fifth oration, seen in this idealistic light of the merger of honor and usefulness, is an interesting and highly practical argument. Given the rather idealistic argument of the previous oration—that education is important for the production of good citizens—the reader may approach this fifth oration expecting that Vico's declared thesis—that states have gained the greatest glory in battle and the greatest political power when they have cultivated letters—to mean something other than it appears to mean. But this is not the case. Given that the University of Naples had undergone a period of reform beginning in 1703, both the previous oration and this one can be seen to address timely topics. But it would be a mistake to explain them away only in historical terms, as though Vico were not also philosophically convinced of the truth of his views. Vico puts his case in terms of the difference between a conception of universal law—what he calls "the divine right of nations" (par. 7)—and the civil law of a particular people. He says: "Man has a dual citizenship, one of which has been given to him by nature, the other by the conditions of his birth. The limits of the former are the heavens, those of the latter are precisely defined" (ibid.).

In civil society, the legal conditions of the individual's existence prevail by common consent. In his later writings on universal law and in the *New Science* Vico would make much of this, in terms of what is established by the power of authority or human will (*auctoritas*) in human affairs. Within civil societies our rights are protected by legal procedures, Vico says, but when the greater fellowship of humanity that is typified by the alliances among nations is violated by a nation, the only resort is to war. It is commonly said that Vico did not become interested in the question of the law of nations until he had accepted the commission to write the life of Antonio Carafa, which caused him to discover and to study the work of Grotius *On the Law of War and Peace* (1625), such as he describes in the autobiography.[29]

He began reading Grotius in 1709, the same year he published the seventh oration. But it is clear from the fifth oration that he was interested in this question earlier, although it could be acknowledged that he is only broaching the issue here—not giving even in outline his conception of universal law, which finally in the *New Science* connects the conception of natural law with the providential development of each nation in terms of its "ideal eternal history" (a cycle of birth, maturity, and fall). But Vico does here insist on the superiority of universal right, as rooted in human nature itself, over the civil rights of a people, those simply decided on by social institutions.

Vico goes on to remind the students that certain forms of knowledge and certain arts are useful and necessary for the successful conduct of war—rhetoric to exhort the populace, architecture for defenses, optics for estimating distance, and so forth. But Vico begins the oration by stressing that prudence, valor, and wisdom are essential for the survival of the nation and that these are part of the education in the liberal arts. He says: "If fortitude is a heroic virtue, then certainly prudence is nearly divine because it knows the changing conditions of fortune and transforms chance into the purposeful" (par. 1).

Finally, Vico argues that great military commanders developed their greatness through their grasp of history and its course, which they acquired in their study of past deeds. Alexander was inspired by his study of Homer's Achilles and Caesar by his study of Alexander. Thus, Vico claims, "we can justly trace the renown of Alexander and Caesar to Homer, which means to say, the literary arts" (par. 11). Vico's point, certainly, is that although we may say that leadership or greatness is a natural quality, real greatness or leadership rests on that natural quality being developed by the study of prudence and wisdom and the virtues, as well as of history, by an

29. *Autobiography*, pp. 154–55.

education in letters. No amount of technical acumen or specialist training will win a war or allow for someone to turn around a moment of social crisis.

Oration VI

The sixth oration is a prelude to the longer seventh (the *Study Methods*) and states clearly the central themes of much of Vico's conception of education in humane letters. It both draws together the themes developed in the previous orations and establishes them as a genuine theory of human education. Because we are by nature human and not divine, we are corrupt, and this natural state of corruption is manifest in "the inadequacy of language, the opinions of the mind, and the passions of the soul" (par. 5). Vico claims that the remedies for these three forms of corruption or error are also three: eloquence, knowledge, and virtue. These are the three points around which education in the arts and sciences circle: "All wisdom is contained in these three most excellent things—to know with certainty, to act rightly, and to speak with dignity" (ibid.). Further on, Vico, paraphrasing Cicero, defines wisdom as "knowledge of things divine and prudent judgment in human affairs and speech that is true and proper" (par. 9). Vico also connects moral doctrine with jurisprudence, or practical wisdom as based in human law or right.

There is no doubt, then, that the aim of education for Vico is the cultivation of the most complete union possible among *sapientia, eloquentia,* and *prudentia.* This is the goal of a true human education. Vico is concerned not only with the goals but with the order of studies, the order in which all the fields of knowledge are to be introduced into the student's experience. Vico's principle is that the course of studies must follow and be attuned to the natural development of the human self. He says that children have strong memories so they should be taught languages because their memory is as strong as their reason is weak (par. 12). He says that adolescents should be introduced to the study of mathematics because it often requires the construction of images. Vico reflects this point in the *Study Methods*, where he distinguishes between

Euclidean geometry, which requires images, and analytic geometry, which should be taught later because of its abstraction.[30] He then sees physics as a subject that can come after mathematics, as the human advances in maturity and can think apart from the body and the senses, because physics deals with abstract entities.

The student, gaining in maturity, moves to metaphysics, a higher level of abstraction, then to moral theology, and finally to prudence in human affairs and jurisprudence, which should be coupled with eloquence. Vico says that these are the subjects that must be learned from teachers—what he calls "esoteric," and he says the histories of all these fields one can learn on one's own because the histories are exoteric—external to the mastery of the subjects themselves.[31]

In his autobiography Vico is proud that he, like Epicurus, was an autodidact, self-taught. He describes how he withdrew from grammar school at an early age to study at home; how he attended the university only slightly, going to hear a lecture of Aquadia on law and for two months to hear privately Verde's teaching of cases. His education was completed by his reading in the library of the Franciscan convent of Santa Maria della Pietà (which contained over three hundred volumes), while he was tutor for nine years to the Rocca family at Vatolla (during which time he formally received a degree in law from the university, without actually attending lectures).[32] Vico writes of his attempt, while too young, to study the abstractions of metaphysics and of how it sent him into a period of dangerous depression—thus illustrating the truth of his theory[33] that the young are unsuited for such abstract and logical studies.

In his autobiography, which Vico wrote while in his late fifties, he presents his own education as autodidactical; in his late thirties, however, he proposed in this sixth oration a system of education based on the need for the crucial part of it to be taught—the

30. *Study Methods*, pp. 6–9, esp. nn. 2 and 3.

31. On the conception of *esoterikoi logoi* and *exoterikoi logoi* as it relates to Aristotle, see A. P. Bos, "The Idea of *Enkyklios Paideia*," *Journal of the History of Ideas* 50 (1989): 179–98.

32. See *New Art of Autobiography*, pp. 190–92.

33. *Autobiography*, p. 113.

esoteric subjects. The solution to this apparent paradox may be that Vico found the system of education of his day to be inadequate, not because it was especially Cartesian in nature but because it was, in many ways, clumsy and boring. Thus it was necessary for him to seek out his own "teachers" in the form of the authors of the various classics of poetry, jurisprudence, and metaphysics that he studied.

It was necessary for him to devise instinctively for himself a program of studies similar, at least in many respects, to that which he later advocates. He is advocating this as an order of studies to be considered within the system of formal education, that is, the university curriculum. But it should be realized that, above all, he is advocating it as a program of study to be taken up by the individual, making use of whatever resources are available. Because Vico's conception of education is based on *paideia*, the actual process of education goes on in the human soul, not simply as a plan for the organization of classrooms and curricula—although surely these should, ideally, be made to coincide.

3

In the *Study Methods*, Vico makes it much clearer that the studies of the young are to be centered first around the arts of rhetoric and poetic, those that train in the art of topics, metaphor, and memory. The education of the young is to be in the powers of the mind that can form images of the world.[34] Early education in abstract conceptual thinking ruins the mind. Although a young mind can be trained to excel in such abstraction, that mind will be ruined because, when mature, although it can make conceptual connections, it will have no facility to form the starting points of arguments and subjects. It will have no skill to make metaphors or to seek common places or topics from which to reason or to invent forms of thought.

---

34. In the *New Science* Vico makes this thought of images the primordial power of collective humanity in his doctrine of "imaginative universals" (*universali fantastici*). For a discussion of "imaginative universals" see my *Vico's Science of Imagination* (1981; rpt. Ithaca: Cornell University Press, 1991), chap. 3.

It has been commonly thought that the *Study Methods* is the beginning of Vico's anti-Cartesian position, even though he does not mention Descartes by name. His full attack on Descartes's conception of knowledge and metaphysics is present in the *Ancient Wisdom*, in 1710, but in that work his topic is not education as such. Fisch, following Nicolini, says the "teaching of Vico's first six inaugural orations (1699–1706) is largely Cartesian."[35] He points to Vico's comment in the third oration that the philologist does not know any more about the customs and ways of ancient Rome than did ordinary people at the time. Fisch sees this as sharing in Descartes's and Malebranche's contempt for history. In the first oration (par. 10), Vico paraphrases an argument of the third *Meditation* of Descartes, that from the existence of the knower as a thinking being can be proved the existence of God. And he accepts in this oration (and in the second) the Stoic dualism between mind and nature typical also of the Cartesian position. But in the same oration he asserts the strongest claims for the humanist ideal of education, using Socrates and Cicero, among others.

Indeed, the third oration is the one in which Descartes is most overtly present. In par. 6 Vico says to the student that he should know how Descartes has meditated on first philosophy and how he has applied geometry to physics. "You will discover," Vico says, "that he is a philosopher like no other." Yet this comes within a long list of thinkers and poets that Vico recommends the student study, from Ovid and Plautus, Virgil, Cicero, Plato, the Stoics, and Descartes, to Galen. Vico is saying that the student can learn

35. Introduction to *Autobiography*, p. 37. As reflected in the inclusive dates for the *Orations* in the above quotation, Fisch, following Nicolini, does not accept Vico's dates for several orations as given in the *Autobiography*. Thus Fisch gives 1699, 1700, 1702, 1703, 1705, and 1706 (see his Chronological Table, on pp. 226–27). Visconti follows Vico's own summaries in the *Autobiography* (pp. 140–45): 1699, 1700, 1701, 1704, 1705, 1707. H. P. Adams, *The Life and Writings of Giambattista Vico* (London: Allen & Unwin, 1935), gives the following reason for holding that the third oration was not delivered in 1701: "No inaugural oration was delivered in 1701. At the time when these orations were usually spoken the city was, in that year, a scene of confusion and alarm. In 1700 the event for which the statesmen of Europe had for years been trying to prepare, the death of the Spanish king, let loose the war which Vico regarded as the modern counterpart of that between Rome and Carthage" (p. 78).

different things from each. But fundamentally what Vico is advocating as a model of education in these orations is not Cartesian. He is not aggressively attacking Descartes as having the precisely wrong conception of knowledge, as he does from at least 1710 on, and, in the *Study Methods*, even a bit earlier. But the view that he was simply a Cartesian must, I think, be modified.

This is my point: *in these first six orations Vico has certainly not identified Descartes as the villain in what is defective with the modern conception of education and theory of knowledge, but the conception of education that Vico propounds is also certainly not Cartesian in nature.*[36] It is derived from sources in the Greek and Latin rhetorical and philosophical traditions and from the Renaissance humanists. These are the figures and texts Vico most often paraphrases and to which he constantly refers. Vico's conception of the order of studies in the sixth oration differs from that of Descartes in the author's letter to the *Principles*, in which he presents an order of the sciences as a tree "whose roots are metaphysics, whose trunk is physics, and whose branches, which issue from the trunk, are all the other sciences."[37] Descartes says that of these sciences there are three principal ones: medicine, mechanics, and morals. He regards moral science as the last degree of wisdom (although he never produced such a science)—as does Vico.

Also, Vico claims that such moral science must be based on the study of moral theology and connected with jurisprudence, which is connected with rhetoric and a knowledge of things human and divine. Vico sees that Descartes's entire order would need to be based on the earlier training of the mind in languages and the construction of images required for mathematics. But even more, Vico has formulated an ideal of human education, fully based on the study of the ancients and on rhetoric, on the interconnection of

36. Vico himself apparently saw these first six orations as at least leading up to his position in the *Study Methods* and did not see the *Study Methods* as a radical break in his thought, or he would not have projected the integration of them into a book (see below, the page of his contents). In his summary of the six orations in his autobiography, Vico omits his references to Descartes, although at this point he is presenting their significance from the standpoint of his developed philosophy.

37. *The Philosophical Works of Descartes*, trans. E. S. Haldane and G. R. T. Ross, 2 vols. (Cambridge: Cambridge University Press, corr. ed. 1931), 1:211.

wisdom, eloquence, and prudence advocated by Cicero in his rhetorical conception of knowledge and furthered by the humanists.[38]

This goes completely against Descartes's claims, in the first part of the *Discourse*, of the uselessness of the search for truth in poetry, rhetoric, and histories and of the distortion of his own early education by such studies. He says that the study of histories and fables makes thinkers "liable to fall into the extravagance of the knights-errant of Romance, and form projects beyond their power of performance"; he says, against eloquence, "Those who have the strongest power of reasoning, and who most skillfully arrange their thought in order to render them clear and intelligible, have the best power of persuasion even if they can but speak the language of Lower Brittany [*bas breton*] and have never learned rhetoric." And Descartes says that he compares "the works of the ancient pagans which deal with Morals to palaces most superb and magnificent, which are yet built on sand and mud alone."[39] This is quite far from and certainly opposite in spirit to anything Vico wishes to endorse—even in these early orations—in which he had not yet declared himself an enemy of Cartesianism.

The Cartesian ideal has won out, basically, in the creation of the goals of modern education, which has excluded rhetoric and poetic as the true basis of thought. With this exclusion, of valuing logic over eloquence, has come the exclusion of wisdom and prudence and virtue as the goals of human education. Vico could see this in his own time, and in his works to follow he made this very clear, saying succinctly, in his 1737 oration to the Academy of Oziosi, near the end of his career: "I hold the opinion that if eloquence does not regain the lustre of the Latins and Greeks in our time, when our sciences have made progress equal to and perhaps even

38. For the sense in which the humanists are to be understood as philosophers, see Ernesto Grassi, *Rhetoric as Philosophy: The Humanist Tradition* (University Park: Pennsylvania State University Press, 1980), and *Renaissance Humanism: Studies in Philosophy and Poetics* (Binghamton, N.Y.: SUNY Center for Medieval and Early Renaissance Studies, 1988).

39. For these three statements, see *Discourse on Method*, Part 1 (*Philosophical Works of Descartes*, 1.85).

greater than theirs, it will be because the sciences are taught completely stripped of every badge of eloquence."[40]

Unless we go back, to recall the ancient and humanist ideal of thought that is rooted in the power of metaphor and memory and of the rhetorical conception of speech and its connection with self-knowledge, no amount of theories of the nature of reading, of the meaning of the texts, of structural, postmodern, or hermeneutical analysis will successfully ground a doctrine of the humanities and of liberal education. The danger for the reader in approaching these six orations is that to read them quickly and superficially is to miss the sense of the ideas that are generated therein. These orations must be read with the footnotes, which supply the references and often the passages that apply for the Greek, Latin, and humanist texts that Vico is directly or indirectly citing or presupposing, which have been selectively supplied by the translators from the footnotes and commentary of Visconti.

Any great thinker causes the reader, in order to understand what has been said, to read or reread and to recall that upon which the thinker's thought is based. In this way any great thinker is a whole university (a trait Vico attributes to the ancients, especially Plato), and Vico is no exception. His purpose is to make his hearers or readers recall or to show them the need to study the great tradition upon which his thoughts are based. As against Descartes's doctrine that thought need only be founded on the logical criterion of *clarté*, Vico, in the *New Science*, sets down the golden principle that "doctrines must take their beginning from that of the matters of which they treat."[41] All books being about other books, Vico's orations are intended to lead us both forward and backward at once. Unless we are put into a motion of this sort we will miss the point of these orations, and they will remain for us flat and shallow. But if we read them with sympathy they will emerge as Vico's own introduction to his philosophy, the true beginning of the path that leads to his great discovery of the new science of the principles of humanity.

40. "The Academies and the Relation between Philosophy and Eloquence," p. 87.
41. *New Science*, par. 314.

Translators' Note

ᡐᢋᢋᢉ

This translation of Giambattista Vico's *Inaugural Orations* is
based on the Latin text edited and annotated by Gian Galeazzo
Visconti, *Le Orazioni Inaugurali, I–VI* (Bologna: Il Mulino,
1982), volume 1 of *Opere di Giambattista Vico* commissioned by
the Centro di Studi Vichiani, directed by Fulvio Tessitore, and
under the patronage of Italy's Consiglio Nazionale delle Ricerche.
The authorization to use this Latin text for the English translation
has been generously granted to the translators by the Director of
the Centro di Studi Vichiani, Naples, Italy.

Visconti's edition is supported by extensive commentary and
footnotes. We have relied heavily on this material. For each of the
orations we have basically reproduced Visconti's citations to classical and humanist texts, occasionally adding references of our
own, which are distinguished by being placed within square brack-
ets. The paragraph enumerations are Visconti's, not Vico's. The
"List of Sources Cited" gives the references to all works cited in
Visconti's text with the corresponding footnote numbers to the
English translation. We have included a General Index, listing the
significant Latin terms that occur in the orations with the English
readings used in the translation.

The meanings of the Latin terms *anima, animus,* and *mens* are traditionally difficult to render into English. We have consistently translated *anima* as "soul," *animus* as "spirit," and *mens* as "mind."

Translators' Note

The general titles of the orations given on their title pages and in the table of contents are not Vico's. They are intended to give the modern reader a preliminary overview of the topics covered. The orations are preceded by the summaries of them that Vico included in his *Autobiography*, in the translation of Max Harold Fisch and Thomas Goddard Bergin (Ithaca: Cornell University Press, 1944).

In the Italian text of his *Autobiography*, Vico gives in Latin the statement of the argument of each oration. Our translations of these arguments (which appear beneath the oration titles and sometimes in the text as well) follow Visconti's edition and vary in some instances from those found in the Fisch and Bergin translation of the summaries, owing to slight differences in Vico's language. Although these may not be identical in mode of expression, they are not intended to differ in meaning.

The dates Vico gives for the delivery of the orations are somewhat problematic. Visconti notes (p. 11n of his 1982 edition) that according to the research of Salvatore Monti, *Sulla tradizione e sul testo delle orazioni inaugurali di Vico* (Naples, 1977), the sequence should be 1699, 1700, 1702, 1705, 1706, and 1707.

We wish to express our gratitude for the encouragement and support received from the Institute for Vico Studies, New York and Atlanta, and its directors, Giorgio Tagliacozzo and Donald Phillip Verene, and from Cornell University Press. We also acknowledge the valuable stylistic suggestions that were given to us by Florence Philbin.

GIORGIO A. PINTON AND ARTHUR W. SHIPPEE

Canton Center, Connecticut

On Humanistic Education

(SIX INAUGURAL ORATIONS, 1699–1707)

On Self-Knowledge

Summary of Oration I

The first [oration], delivered the 18th of October 1699, proposes that we cultivate the force of our divine mind in all its faculties. Its thesis is: "That the knowledge of oneself is for each of us the greatest incentive to the compendious study of every branch of learning [in the shortest possible time]." It proves that the human mind is by analogy the god of man, just as God is the mind of the whole [of things]. It shows severally how the marvelous faculties of the mind, whether senses or imagination or memory or invention or reason, perform with divine powers of quickness, facility and efficiency the most numerous and varied tasks at one and the same time. How children, free of evil affections and vices, at the end of three or four years of idle play are found to have learned the entire vocabulary of their native tongues. How Socrates did not so much bring down moral philosophy from heaven as elevate our spirit to it, and how those who for their inventions were raised to heaven among the gods are but the intelligence which each of us possesses. How it is a matter for astonishment that there should be so many ignorant persons when ignorance or being misled or falling into error is as repugnant to the mind as smoke is to the eyes, or a foul stench to the nose; wherefore negligence is especially to be condemned. How it is only because we do not wish to be that we are not instructed in everything, seeing that by our efficacious will alone, when transported by inspiration, we do things which when accomplished we wonder at as if they had been done not by ourselves but by a god. And therefore it concludes that if in a few years a youth has not run through the whole round of the sciences it is only because he did not want to, or if he had the desire he has failed for lack of teachers or of a good order of study, or because the end of his studies was something other than cultivating a kind of divinity in our mind. [*Autobiography*, pp. 140–41]

On Self-Knowledge

ᘓᗒᘏᗕᘒ

ORATION I

(Given on October 18, 1699. Argument: "Knowledge of oneself is for everyone the greatest incentive to acquire the universe of learning in the shortest possible time.")

[1]   Certainly "many traditions have been wisely discovered and instituted by our ancestors"[1] for the moral well-being and the happiness of the society founded upon them. None, however, is more excellent than having decided to hold a convocation at the beginning of the academic year after the summer vacation in order to exhort our youth to resume their studies with an alert and dedicated disposition. For our nature is so constituted that men are inclined to leisure rather than to labor and they shun difficulties and pursue easy things. It has become clear, then, that we have the duty to convince the youth by argument to take up the studies of the liberal arts and sciences, which can be acquired only with strong dedication of the mind, with long and late hours of application, with sweat, with persistent discipline, and with punctilious diligence. So it is that the fruits we enjoy in our peaceful society are for the most part based on the cultivation of these studies, which, like trees in their seed, are all contained, I dare say, in this most advantageous tradition. Moreover, the most happy natural disposition of this age, and especially in this common-

1. Cicero *Concerning His House* 1.

35

Vico addressing young men (16-17 yr olds) matriculating in University

wealth, is such, by good fortune, that from earliest youth men are seized with a certain marvelous and incredible desire for learning. Also, they do not aspire merely to a kind of popular and superficial erudition for pure ostentation but strive with discipline and dedicated diligence to acquire a clearer, deeper, varied, and manifold understanding of things.[2]

[2] All this came suddenly to my mind when, a few days ago, I was assigned the duty of giving this exhortation by the Chancellor of the University, who has the authority, for the time being, to make this assignment. By rights, I could have refused the assignment because it had been imposed upon me in a quite improper and unusual manner; nevertheless, I accepted it willingly, thinking that it would be neither hard, nor wearisome, nor difficult. I thought that it would even be easy for a man however lacking in eloquence and naive in speech to incite by an oration the youth that have come here already so well motivated to listen so that they might seek after the study of the liberal arts without limits and manifest a praiseworthy boundless enthusiasm. I realized, however, that my greatest desire to please such an eminent personage brought me, and forced me, into this choice without any time for reflection. Later, in fact, while I calmly examined my decision to agree, clear thinking not only failed to find arguments suitable to encourage me, rather those very arguments appeared to discourage me even from what I had already started. You, O youths of great natural ability, are in truth not like those whom it is necessary to attract by arguments to the study of wisdom, since you are already dedicated to those studies, in which, if one looks for advantages, there are none greater; if one looks for satisfaction, there is none more pleasurable and sweeter; if one looks for fame and honor, there is none more illustrious, solid, and abiding in making one's name immortal. Of course, you brought these convictions here with you from home and, therefore, value them as commonplace and obvious. On this occasion you certainly expect from me

watch for irony

2. Cicero *Orator* 163: "one should select the most euphonious words, but they must not be selected with particular attention to euphony as the poets do, but taken from the ordinary language"; see also Horace *Art of Poetry* 243.

a discourse about something greater, since above all, you are not of a timid spirit, one which accepts limitations, one which is content with only one kind of doctrine and is easily convinced by it. Indeed, so wonderful a passion for knowledge is shared among you, let us admit, that you consider no one a scholar who is not excellently learned in the entire universe of studies.[3] And this even to the extent that there is no discipline which he has not mastered to perfection and learned so thoroughly that he conveys the impression of having applied himself all his life to that single discipline alone.

[3]   What then would I myself have to offer you worthy of your expectations, O listeners, that would not be less than what you hope for and, at the same time, would satisfy the dignity of the scholars among you? How would I satisfy the noble spirits of this youth? What would be suitable to this most sacred sanctuary of wisdom? What would be fitting to be spoken in this most spacious and splendid lecture hall, which I now approach for the first time ready to speak although without experience? This crowded gathering, together with your complete attention and the great zeal expressed on your faces and in your eyes, brings me out of my reluctance and not only gives me confidence and strength for what I wish to accomplish but also encourages and lifts me up to seek lofty goals. And thus I will dare to offer you today an argument that by itself will be sufficient to make each of you aware, not only of being capable, but also of being sufficiently gifted in most effectively acquiring the knowledge of all branches of the liberal arts and sciences. As a sphere rotates on its axis, so does my argument hinge on this: knowledge of oneself is for everyone the greatest

3. See Quintilian *Rules of Rhetoric* I.10.1: "I will now proceed briefly to discuss the remaining arts in which I think boys ought to be instructed before being handed over to the teacher of rhetoric: for it is by such studies that the course of education described by the Greeks as 'egkuklios paideia' or general education will be brought to its full completion." See also Vitruvius *On Architecture* I.8.12: "So they began to come down, one at a time, and to meet with society, and thus they were brought back of their own accord, giving up their rough and savage ways for the delights of Greek customs. Hence . . . those barbarians were softened by the charm of civilization" [*Vitruvius. The Ten Books on Architecture*, trans. Morris Hicky Morgan (New York: Dover, 1960), p. 55].

incentive to acquire the universe of learning in the shortest possible time. Therefore, you, the flower and stock of well-born young manhood to whom my speech is principally directed, give me your attention. Relying on your goodwill I hope to treat the argument in such a way that this day may be seen to have obtained for me the reward of a deed excellently done and for you a yield of enormous benefit.

[4] Among the many wisest precepts that are practiced in order to achieve happiness in life, the one that seems to have been made totally for that purpose and stands in every way as the most important is expressed in two short words and has been immortalized by antiquity in golden letters on Apollo's temple in Delphi. This is: "Know thyself."[4] This saying was so renowned, so praised, that many tried to attribute it to Pythagoras, many to Thales of Miletus, others to Bias, others to Chilon of Sparta, all men traditionally reputed to be the most distinguished pillars of human wisdom. However, because this precept contains in such brevity of words so great an abundance of good fruit that nothing excelled it, it was not long reputed to be from these men though they were the wisest, and instead was attributed by unanimous consensus to the Pythian oracle. The celebrity of this saying could not be as great as is commonly thought if formulated to subdue pride of spirit and cast down human arrogance, since innumerable and almost infinite proofs of human frailty and misery are available everywhere.[5] Let the most eloquent of the wise men, or the wisest of the eloquent men, Cicero, come forth and explain the

4. Plato *Philebus* 48c; *Charmides* 164e-165a: "For I would almost say that self-knowledge is the very essence of temperance, and in this I agree with him who dedicated the inscription 'Know thyself!' at Delphi. That inscription, if I am not mistaken, is put there as a sort of salutation which the god addresses to those who enter the temple—as much as to say that the ordinary salutation of 'Hail!' is not right, and that the exhortation 'Be temperate!' is far better. . . . This, however, like a prophet, he expresses in a sort of riddle, for 'Know thyself!' and 'Be temperate!' are the same, as I maintain, and as the words imply, and yet they may be thought to be different"; *Protagoras* 343b; *Hipparchus or Greater Hippias* 282e: "Socrates, you know nothing. . . ."

5. See Cicero *To Quintus, His Brother* III.5.7: "You must not rest on your oars and you must not be under the idea that the well-known *nosce teipsum* was only meant to apply to the abatement of arrogance[; it] also means that we should recognize our own gifts."

divine force of that saying with his sublime tongue: " 'Know thyself.' This means 'Know your own spirit.' The body is, indeed, like
a vessel or a shelter of the spirit; whatever is done by you is done
by your spirit. Unless the precept to know the spirit were not from
a divine command, how then could it possess such a profound
meaning? It certainly could not be anything other than the command of a superior mind. Therefore, it was attributed to God."6
M. Tullius has sufficiently illustrated this precept so that we can
understand what this wisest of sayings means. Man, who by lack
of courage constrains his divine mind, by lack of confidence in
himself debases it, and by despair of great accomplishments wears

6. Cicero *Tusculan Disputations* I.52: "It is a point of the utmost importance
to realize that the soul sees by means of the soul alone, and surely this is the
meaning of Apollo's maxim advising that each one should know himself. For I do
not suppose the meaning of the maxim is that we should know our limbs, our
height or shape; our selves are not bodies, and in speaking as I do to you, I am not
speaking to your body. When then Apollo says, 'Know thyself,' he says, 'Know thy
soul.' " See also Plato *Alcibiades* I.124a: "O my friend, be persuaded by me, and
hear the Delphian inscription, 'Know thyself'"; Cicero *Tusc.* V.70; *On the Greatest
Good* III.73; V.44; *On Laws* I.58.61. [Marsilio Ficino *Preface to Platonic Theology on the Immortality of Souls* I.15–17: "that oracular saying 'know thyself' most
potently urges that whoever wished to know God should first know himself"
Marsilio Ficino: *Books of Epistles* I.1 in *Marsilii Ficini Florentini, insignis philoso-
phi Platonici, medici atque theologi clarissimi Opera . . . Basileae, anno 1561*, p.
659, 34.]
Vico's quotations from and references to Cicero's *Tusculan Disputations* refer to
an edition of the *Tusculanae Disputationes* published in Paris in 1549 with the
erroneous title *Tusculanarum Quaestionum Libri V*. One copy of this edition was
found by Gian Galeazzo Visconti in the Fondo Valletta della Biblioteca Oratoriana
dei Girolamini. In fact, Giuseppe Valletta's (1636–1714) celebrated library and
salon was one of the most famous in Naples. The library was much the best in the
city during Vico's youth, and he had access to it. Years after the death of Giuseppe
Valletta, his heirs had the library appraised by Vico and sold it in 1726 to the
Fathers of the Oratory. [For this information see Fisch in the introduction to the
Autobiography, p. 33.] Vico, then, must have had access to the Parisian edition of
Cicero's work at the Valletta Library. That he used this edition is confirmed by the
following facts: (A) Commenting on the *gnothi seauton,* Vico repeats a polemic
thought expressed by Cicero to his brother Quintus (III.5.7). (B) Vico quotes the
passage of the *Tusculanae Disputationes* I.52 exactly as it appears in the Paris
edition, even with the errors of transcription there contained. (C) In reference to
Tusc. I.73, Vico uses the construction *se ipsam intuens,* which appears only in the
Paris edition, instead of the common *se ipsa intuens.*(D) Referring to *Tusc.* I.38,
Vico quotes again directly from the Paris edition, using the term *revocare* instead of
sevocare, which appears in other editions and in classical authors who cite this
passage.

it down, may instead be incited and encouraged to undertake great and sublime endeavors for which he has a more than ample capacity. Know thyself, therefore, O youth, so that you can attain wisdom, since you are born for wisdom.

[5] "But—you say—it requires a great effort of character to keep one's own mind free from its accustomed ways and in control of the senses."[7] Agreed. But great successes are in truth only the products of equally great efforts. Have courage, then, and know thyself: know your spirit, and you will acknowledge how admirable, how exceptional, how uncommon you will have known it to be, unless you wish to deceive yourself. "The acuity of the mind, to whatever degree, can penetrate all other matters, but becomes dull when considering itself."[8] Also, in the same effort to know yourself, you perceive the divinity of your own spirit and recognize that it is the image of Almighty God.[9] As God is known by those things that have been created and are contained within this universe, so the spirit is recognized as divine by reason, in which it is preeminent, and by its sagacity, ability, memory, and ingenuity.[10] The spirit is the most manifest image of God. As God is in the world, so the spirit is in the human body. As God is diffused in the elements of the world, so the spirit is diffused throughout the members of the human body.[11] Both are free of all materiality,

---

7. Cicero *Tusc.* I.38; see also Plato *Phaedo* 67c–d: "So this journey which is now ordained for me carries a happy prospect for any other man also who believes that his mind has been prepared by purification . . . And purification . . . , consists in separating the soul as much as possible from the body, and accustoming it to withdraw from all contact with the body and concentrate itself by itself, and to have its dwelling, so far as it can, both now and in the future, alone by itself, freed from the shackles of the body." Cicero *On the Nature of the Gods* II.45; *Scipio's Dream* 29.

8. Cicero *Tusc.* I.73: "in thinking attentively about the soul we suffer the same experience as often comes from gazing intently at the setting sun, that is of losing entirely the sense of sight; in the same way the mind's vision, in gazing upon itself sometimes waxes dim, and for that reason we relax the steadiness of contemplation." See also ibid. I.67; Lactanctius *On the Craftmanship of God* 16 = *Lucii Coelii Lactantii Firmiani Opera . . . Lugd. Batavorum, apud Franciscum Hackium et Petrum Leffen, 1660.*

9. See Cicero *On Laws* I.59: "Well, when you are angry, do you allow your anger to rule your mind?"

10. See Cicero *Tusc.* I.67: ". . . power, wisdom, memory, rapidity of movement. These things are of real moment, these are divine, these are everlasting."

11. See Lactanctius *On the Craftmanship of God* 16.

and, unmixed with any corporality, they act in their purity.[12] As God is present throughout the world, so the spirit is present throughout the body, but neither is God limited by the world nor the spirit by the body. God, indeed, makes all constellations rotate within the ethereal sphere, hurls thunderbolts from the heavens, moves the storms at sea, and on the earth brings forth all things. But neither the heavens, nor the sea, nor the earth constitutes God's only throne. The human mind in the ear hears, in the eye sees, in the stomach shows anger, in the spleen laughs, in the heart discerns, and in the brain understands; but still it has no definite shrine in any part of the body. God embraces all things; He reigns over all things. Outside of Him there is nothing.[13] The spirit, as Sallust says, is "the ruler of all mankind; it moves and possesses all things, but is possessed by none."[14] God is continuous activity, the spirit is continuous productivity. The world is because God is; if the world should end, God will still be. The body experiences because the spirit activates it. You may kill the body, but the spirit is immortal. Finally, God is the master artist of nature; the mind, we may say, is the god of the arts. O matchless excellence of the

12. See Cicero *Tusc.* I.66: "'No beginning of souls can be discovered on earth; for there is no trace of blending or combination in souls or any particle. . . . For in these elements there is nothing to possess the power of memory, thought, reflection, nothing capable of retaining the past, or foreseeing the future and grasping the present, and these capacities are nothing but divine; and never will there be found any source from which they can come to men except from God. . . . And indeed God Himself, who is comprehended by us, can be comprehended in no other way save as mind unfettered and free, severed from all perishable matter, conscious of all and moving all and self-endowed with perpetual motion.' Of such sort and of the same nature is the human mind." Augustine *City of God* XXII.20: "For it was into a face of earth that God breathed the breath of life when man was made a living soul; as if it were said, Thou art earth with a soul, which thou wast not; thou shalt be earth without a soul, as thou wast" [trans. Marcus Dods (New York: Modern Library, 1950)]; Marsilio Ficino *Books of Epistles* I.1 = *Opera* p. 659, 34–36.
13. See Marsilio Ficino *Platonic Theology* XV.5 in *Opera* p. 337, 47: "the whole soul is in every little part of the body." See also Plotinus *Enneads* V.1.2, VI.4.12.
14. Sallust *The War with Jugurtha* 2.3: "In short, the goods of the body and of fortune have an end as well as a beginning, and they all rise and fall, wax and wane; but the mind, incorruptible, eternal, ruler of mankind, animates and controls all things, yet is itself not controlled." See also Plato *The Laws* 896b–c: "soul . . . it has disclosed itself as the universal cause of all changes and motion? . . . Soul is prior to body, body secondary and derivative, soul governing in the real order of things, and body being subject to governance."

spirit that cannot be explained suitably and aptly except by its similarity to Almighty God![15] Once you have known to what the spirit is similar, you have known its very nature. The spirit, indeed, is a certain divine force of thought. O Immortal God, how great is the spirit's speed, how swift all its motions! How like a flame! How varied, diverse, and multiple are its functions! How abundant its skillfulness and ingenuity! Would that Minerva had given me a gift of language so profound and so rich that I could explain with my words the attributes of the spirit as you have already done so with your thought!

[6] I will, therefore, only briefly mention them and you will be judge of how wonderfully great they are. First of all, how is it that in one and the same instant we apprehend through the senses, used as messengers, qualities that are absolutely dissimilar? Yet in each one of these qualities, according to their kind, how is it that the mind, like the strictest judge, succeeds in distinguishing so many differences that the more it discovers of them the less it is able to describe them? In fact, has there ever been a language so flourishing in words that it could express each individual color with a precise name, or each flavor with a word indicating its uniqueness, or that could describe each aroma with more than a few unsuitable terms? Truly, the power that fashions the images of things, which is called phantasy, at the same time that it originates and produces new forms, reveals and confirms its own divine origin.[16] It was this that imagined the gods of all major and minor nations;[17] it was this that imagined the heroes; it is this that now

15. See Cicero *Tusc.* V.38.

16. [We have rendered *phantasia* here and throughout as "phantasy" to remain cognate to the Latin (see Oration I.6; II.6, 14; IV.2; VI.13) and to distinguish it from *imaginatio*, which we have translated as "imagination." Later, in the *New Science*, the Italian *fantasia* becomes the central term of Vico's conception of "poetic wisdom" (*sapienza poetica*) and of "imaginative universals" (*universali fantastici*), upon which much of his conception of history and knowledge is based. In their translation of the *New Science* Bergin and Fisch render *fantasia* as "imagination." We have used "phantasy" to preserve the sense that the term has not yet become special for Vico. "Phantasy" as a form of illusory thinking or falsehood is not what Vico means. Rather, he understands *phantasia* as our power to form images and as closely associated with memory. On "imaginative universals" see Donald Phillip Verene, *Vico's Science of Imagination* (Ithaca: Cornell University Press, 1991; orig. pub. 1981), chap. 3.—*Trans.*]

17. Vico mentions the distinction in Roman religion between *maiores* and *mi-*

differentiates the forms of things, sometimes separating them, at other times mixing them together. It is phantasy that makes present to our eyes lands that are very far away, that unites those things that are separated, that overcomes the inaccessible, that discloses what is hidden and builds a road through trackless places. And it does all this with unbelievable swiftness! I would just mention the land of Magellan, and you have already walked there. I may just have indicated "Novaya Zemlya," and you have already arrived there. I would just name an ocean and you have already crossed it by swimming; I would just refer to the firmament and you, using the poet's words, have already gone beyond "the wall of the universe."[18] And still, in spite of this power, we prefer to marvel at the sun's cycle of twenty-four hours and at nations that lament and protest their month-long nights!

----

nores gods, a distinction relevant to the comprehension of the successive development of Vichian thought concerning the relation between the aristocracy and the populace. The *maiores* gods (Juno, Vesta, Minerva, Ceres, Diana, Venus, Mars, Mercury, Jupiter, Neptune, Vulcan, and Apollo) were venerated by the wealthiest and most educated persons, *gentes maiores* (patricians). The *minores* gods (Hercules, Castor and Pollux, Liber or Lyaeus, Aesculapius) were men who, for their distinction and merits, were elevated to the heavens by the *gentes minores* (plebeians). Vico expands these ideas in the *New Science*, pars. 317, 392, 734. See Lactanctius *Divine Institutes* I.24. See also Cicero *On Laws* II.19: "They shall worship as gods, both those who have always been regarded as dwellers in heavens, and also those whose merits have admitted them in heaven"; *Tusc.* I.29; *On The Nature of Gods* II.62: "Those gods therefore who were the authors of various benefits owed their deification to the value of the benefits which they bestowed. . . . Human experience moreover and general custom have made it a practice to confer the deification of renown and gratitude upon distinguished benefactors. This is the origin of Hercules, of Castor and Pollux, of Aesculapius, . . . And these benefactors were duly deemed divine, as being both supremely good and immortal, because their souls survived and enjoyed eternal life." Augustine *City of God* VIII.5.

18. Lucretius *On the Nature of Things* I.73: "Therefore the lively power of his mind prevailed, and forth he marched far beyond the flaming walls of the heavens, as he traversed the immeasurable universe in thought and imagination; whence victorious he returns bearing his prize, the knowledge." During the seventeenth century the studies and findings of geography had an exceptional period of growth. On the subject see the descriptions given by Stephanus Morinus in *Dissertatio de Paradiso Terrestri*, in *Samuelis Bocharti Opera Omnia*, . . . *Lugduni Batavorum* . . . *apud Guilielmum vande Water, 1692*, which deal with Australia, Thule, Iceland, Greenland, the Moscovian coasts, Novaya Zemlya, and the northern shores of modern Russia. Later, in the *De Mente Heroica* ["On The Heroic Mind," trans. Elizabeth Sewell and Anthony C. Sirignano, *Social Research* 43 (Winter 1976), 886–903], Vico himself, impressed by these discoveries, exclaims: ". . . and geography how marvelously expanded!" (p. 901).

[7] Be aware that these are the least wonders that we can express of the divine force of the human mind! Indeed, how keen is the faculty of perceiving! How active that of composing and discriminating! How swift that of reasoning![19] Even as I set forth this metaphor, so much valued by Aristotle, and call the cup of wine "the shield of Bacchus," how many and how fast are the combinations, faster than my words, that form themselves within your minds![20] Each of you sees Bacchus and Mars, and next, the cup and the shield. Then you see Mars and the shield and Bacchus and the cup. This is followed by Mars armed with the shield and Bacchus holding the cup. Then you place each of the four in its proper sphere, Mars and Bacchus in the heavens, the shield and the cup here below. After having considered all possible uses of the two objects, you determine their proper use. The shield defends against the enemy as the full cup does against thirst. And, continuing the analogy, Mars uses the shield to conquer the enemy as Bacchus uses the cup to conquer thirst. Afterward, the sides are exchanged and both objects are seen as members of the class of round things. The four elements are then combined in diametrical opposition. At the right there is Bacchus with the shield and at the left Mars with the cup. Finally, you conclude that the shield is the cup of Mars and the cup is the shield of Bacchus.

[8] How much less than what is due to the excellent activity of the spirit have you been able to disclose, O philosophy, who reckons among the work of the mind its immediate perceptions while in such activity there seem to be so many different compositions and ratiocinations! Also, the power by which the human mind compares things together or distinguishes them one from another is so great that neither the most eloquent orator nor I would ever

19. See Cicero *On the Greatest Good* II.45: "For among the many points of difference between man and the lower animals, the greatest difference is that Nature has bestowed on man the gift of Reason, of an active, vigorous intelligence, able to carry on several operations at the same time with extreme speed, and having, so to speak, a keen scent to discern the causes and effects of things, to draw analogies, combine things separate, connect the future with the present, and survey the entire field of the subsequent course of life." Lactanctius *Divine Institutes* VII.8; Marsilio Ficino *Platonic Theology* XIII.3, in *Opera* p. 297, 23–25.
20. See Aristotle *Poetics* 1457b, 20–22.

be able to express its dexterity and skillfulness. Indeed, what may explain the fact that with one single act of perception of the eyes we can see ugliness or deformity in things? Is it not that same power by which, for example, we can inspect all the members of the human body, compare the one with the other, order them, and see how harmoniously they are related? We can, then, determine what is fitting, what is alien, what is missing, what is best. Thus the judgments that in an instant are formulated by the mind are as many as the parts of the body (which are indeed almost infinite). How, moreover, can anyone explain the fact that as soon as the spirit reaches the age of reason, of which it has always been a part, it can now use that very reason to awaken within itself religious feelings toward Almighty God? Why? It has known itself!

[9] Truly, indeed, divine philosophy constructs an extended series of long arguments, deducing the one from the other in such a way that one follows the other and thus explains (and this is almost too audacious to say!) how man, from the knowledge of himself, gradually ascends to that of God. Pay attention to my speech a little longer, O audience, and let us hear the philosophy that shows and confirms the divinity of our mind.

[10] Though the human mind can be uncertain and doubtful about all things, it can in no way doubt that it thinks. Indeed, that very indecision is thinking. Since it cannot deny being conscious of its own thinking, it is from this consciousness of thinking that it derives, in the first place, that it is something. If it were nothing, how could it think? From this it senses within itself an awareness of something infinite. Assuming that there should be in a cause as much as there is in the effect produced by that cause, it further deduces that this awareness of an infinite thing must come from a thing that is itself infinite. At this point man recognizes himself as finite and imperfect, and thus he concludes that that awareness of the infinite originated in him by that which is itself infinite and of which he himself is only a small part. Moving from here he assumes that that which is infinite must encompass all things and nothing should be excluded from it. Thus man concludes that his awareness of the infinite has been implanted in him by the most perfect nature of all. He further assumes that that which is the

most perfect is the culmination of all perfections. Thus no perfection is absent from it. But to exist is a perfection; therefore, man finally concludes that God exists. Also, given that God is all things, he justly deserves all devotion. Oh, marvelous power of the human mind that by a reflection upon itself brings us to the knowledge of the supreme good, Almighty God![21]

[11] Someone among you will, perhaps, wonder about such things and will swear that he himself had never as a young man, let alone as a child, arrived at the knowledge of God by this chain of reasoning. Yes, indeed, he had arrived at it but paid no attention to it. Any one of you can look at paintings daily but may not see the innumerable features observed by artists. Every day any one of you may listen to music and songs, but "how very much he would miss of that to which one skilled in those arts would be sensitive"![22] Why is this, why? Because he has not yet developed the art of looking at pictures or of listening to music. Each of you as a child could have been trained to become the greatest of philosophers, but because you had not been exposed to philosophy, you would not have been aware of it. Truly, all philosophers, historians, orators, and poets have achieved eternal praise among us as men of highest learning for no other reason than that they have earned excellence for having worked harder and more diligently than others in those disciplines, to which they were inclined by the nature of the human spirit. Such, as we have seen, is the swiftness of the mind's power of ratiocination that it is similar to a spinning top which, the more it spins, the more it appears to stand still.

[12] But why am I explaining something of such excellence with a ludicrous metaphor? Why do I not instead compare the mind to the sun, the greatest source of inexhaustible light, which,

21. The entire paragraph constitutes a concise summary of René Descartes's *Meditations on the First Philosophy*, especially "Meditation III." Giovanni Gentile speaks of the "Platonic Cartesianism" of the young Vico in *Studi Vichiani*, 3d ed. (Florence: Sansoni, 1968), pp. 54–56.

22. Cicero *Academica Priora (Lucullus)* 20: "But when we add practice and artistic training, to make our eyes sensitive to painting and our ears to music, who is there who can fail to remark the power that the senses possess? How many things painters see in shadows and in the foreground which we do not see! How many things in music that escape us are caught by the hearing of persons trained."

when at night, it seems to rest, accomplishes, on the contrary, its longest journey? But "I admire memory even more than phantasy."[23] What, indeed, is there more admirable and more divine than the most copious treasure chest of words and ideas of things in the human mind?[24] And, O God Immortal, how quickly we can increase this wealth! By the age of two or three we have acquired by heart all of the words and ideas that constitute everything that is necessary for a daily common life. If a lexicographer should wish to write down all of these words, he would have to compile several large volumes! And what about those skills that brought to man a unique advantage, or great admiration from others, or self-satisfaction? Did not the pagans, though lacking self-knowledge, attribute all of these skills to the gods, or think of them at least as gifts from the gods? Demosthenes called the laws a gift of the gods, because by them the life of society is preserved.[25] In truth, laws are the gift of a human spirit similar to yours. Socrates is said to have derived his moral philosophy from the heavens.[26] On the

23. Cicero *Tusc.* I.59.

24. See Augustine *Confessions* X.8: "So I shall also pass above this power of my nature, ascending by degrees toward Him who made me, and I come into the fields and broad palaces of memory, where there are treasures of innumerable images, brought in from all sorts of sense objects. There is stored away whatever we cogitate on, too, either by adding to, or taking away from, or changing in any way the things which sense perception has contacted, and anything else kept or put back there, which forgetfulness has not yet engrossed and buried. When I am in it, I can request that whatever I wish be brought forward. Some things come forth immediately; others are hunted after for a longer time, yet they are dug out as it were from some more concealed containers; still others rush out in a mob, when something else is sought and looked for, jumping forth in the middle" [*Fathers of the Church*, ed. R. Deferrari et al. (Washington, D.C.: Catholic University of America Press, 1960–)]. See also ibid. X.14.

25. Marcianus Capella *On the Laws and the Decrees of the Senate and on the Established Practice* I.3.2; see also Demosthenes (Pseudo-) *Orations* 25.16.

26. See Cicero *Tusc.* V.10: "Socrates on the other hand was the first to call philosophy down from the heavens and set her in the cities of men and bring her also into their homes and compel to ask questions about life and morality and things good and evil." See also Cicero *Academica (Varro)* 15: "Then Varro began as follows: 'It is my view, and it is universally agreed, that Socrates was the first person who summoned philosophy away from the mysteries veiled in concealment by nature herself, upon which all philosophers before him had been engaged, and led it to the subject of ordinary life, in order to investigate the virtues and vices, and good and evil generally, and to realize that heavenly matters are either remote from our knowledge or else, however fully known, have nothing to do with the good

contrary, he raised man's spirit up to the heavens. Greece attributed medicine to Apollo and eloquence to Mercury, but they were men like you.[27] The lyre of Orpheus and the ship of Argus, when considered as constellations in the sky, confirm with abundant proof that your human minds are of a celestial nature. To be brief, all of the gods, for whatever benefit they have conferred on human society, which antiquity has thus depicted as being in the heavens, are in truth you.[28] O wonderful knowledge of oneself! How high you exalt and honor us! For each one of you, O listeners, the mind is to you your own god. Divine is the faculty that sees; divine that which hears; divine that which conceives ideas; divine that which perceives; divine that which judges; divine that which reasons; divine that which remembers.[29] To see, to hear, to discover, to compare, to infer, to recollect are divine.[30] Sagacity, keenness, cleverness, capability, ingenuity, and swiftness are marvelous, great, and divine.

---

life.'" Francis Bacon *De Dignitate et Augmentis Scientiarum I* [in *The Works of Francis Bacon*, in 10 vols. (London, 1819), 7:85–86]: "Socrates is said to have called philosophy down from heavens and set her on earth, that is, to have put apart physics so that only moral and political philosophy be celebrated. But in the same way that heavens and earth come together and agree in defending and helping human nature, so the goal of both philosophies should be that of preserving all that is fundamental and important to man, rejecting all vain speculation and what is of no value and sterile. Thus, science . . . will be like a spouse (to philosophy) for the generation of honest and advantageous fruits."

27. See Cicero *Tusc.* III.1; Pliny *Natural History* XXIX.1, 2; Horace *Odes* I.10.1–3.

28. *Psa.* 82:6 (Vulgate 81:6): "I have said, Ye are gods, and all of you are children of the most High"; see also Giovanni Pico Della Mirandola *On the Dignity of Man* [trans. Charles Glenn Wallis, Library of Liberal Arts (Indianapolis: Bobbs-Merrill, 1965), p. 7]; Marsilio Ficino *Books of Epistles* I.1; Cicero *Scipio's Dream* 26: "Know, then, that you are god!"; *Cato the Elder. On Old Age* 81: "Again, you really see nothing resembling death so much as sleep; and yet it is when the body sleeps that the soul most clearly manifests its divine nature; for when it is unfettered and free it sees many things that are to come. Hence we know what the soul's future state will be when it has been wholly released from the shackles of the flesh. Wherefore, if what I have said be true, *cherish me as you would a god.* But on the other hand, if my soul is going to perish along with my body, still you, who revere the gods as the guardians and rulers of this beautiful universe, will keep me in loving and sacred memory" [emphasis added].

29. See Plato (Pseudo-) *Axiochus* 365e; Cicero *Tusc.* I.65, 66, V.38; Pliny *Natural History* II.5, 14; Lactantius *Divine Institutes* VII.22.

30. Pliny *Natural History* XXXVII.2, 7; see Cicero *Tusc.* I.67.

[13] If, then, things are thus and man is endowed by nature with so many and great means to achieve wisdom, why is it that he is impeded and held back from the most excellent studies of the liberal arts and sciences? My astonishment is even greater because man's propensity is to search for truth.[31] This, after all, is the reason why every day we wish to see, to hear, and to learn, and we are overcome by the deepest pleasure whenever we succeed in apprehending in new and obscure things that which is certain and distinct. Nature, indeed, has made us for truth, natural disposition guides us, and wonder keeps us persistent. My astonishment thus persists when I further realize that there are so many people ignorant of themselves that they are unaware that as smoke offends the eyes, harsh noise the ears, stench the nose, so to err, to be ignorant, and to be deceived are inimical to the human mind.[32] Such men have never known themselves. They neglect the divine power of the spirit. They do not know in what they can excel. Therefore, they remain deprived and unenlightened concerning the highest truths because they have never ventured by using the faculties of the spirit as wings for soaring upward to divine things. If others "can because

[handwritten margin notes: Aristotle's Poetics / wonder is the beginning of knowledge]

31. Cicero *On Duties* I 13: "Above all, the search after truth and its eager pursuit are peculiar to man. And so, when we have leisure from the demands of business cares, we are eager to see, to hear, to learn something new, and we esteem a desire to know the secret or wonders of creation as indispensable to a happy life. Thus we come to understand that what is true, simple, and genuine appeals most strongly to a man's nature. To this passion for discovering truth there is added a hungering, as it were, for independence, so that a mind well-moulded by Nature is unwilling to be subject to anybody save one who gives rules of conduct or is a teacher of truth or who, for the general good, rules according to justice and law. From this attitude come greatness of soul and a sense of superiority to worldly conditions."

32. Ibid. I.18: "the knowledge of truth, touches human nature most closely. For we are all attracted and drawn to a zeal for learning and knowing; and we think it glorious to excel therein, while we count it base and immoral to fall into error, to wander from truth, to be ignorant, to be led astray." Ibid. I.94: "what, in Latin, may be called *decorum* (propriety) . . . is inseparable from moral goodness; for what is proper is morally right, and what is morally right is proper. The nature of the difference between morality and propriety can be more easily felt than expressed. For whatever propriety may be, it is manifested only when there is pre-existing moral rectitude. . . . For to employ reason and speech rationally, to do with careful consideration whatever one does, and in everything to discern the truth and to uphold it—that is proper. To be mistaken, on the other hand, to miss the truth, to fall into error, to be led astray—that is improper as to be deranged and lose one's mind. And all things just are proper; all things unjust . . . improper."

they thought that they could,"[33] why is it that we, who can, do not think that we could? Let us find out by experience, then, what we are capable of doing, and we will easily achieve what we have the power to achieve. Let us stir up so many important ideas, which are hidden in our minds like sparks under the ashes, implanted, and as it were, grafted on us by the First Truth, that we will kindle a great burning for all learning.[34] The passage is well-known in which Plato narrates the story of Socrates and the slave boy who, replying little by little to all of the easiest and most self-evident short arguments presented by the philosopher, arrived at the geometrical proof of the area of the square though he had absolutely no awareness of geometry.[35] All sciences, yes, all of them, O most fortunate young men, are yours if you rightly know yourselves! Nothing remains to do but to devote your minds to them. O! The overwhelming shame of those who are indolent—not to be wise! Why? Because they have not willed though it is clear that becoming wise depends solely on the will! The poets celebrate its power and efficacy and with the help of phantasy dedicate themselves completely to grasping sublime and noble things. And after setting down those verses by effort of the will, exhausted, they realize that the inspiration of the spirit, like a soft wind, has ceased. They now barely recognize their own work and suppose it to be the product of some higher mind.[36]

33. Virgil *Aeneid* V.231.
34. Cicero *Tusc.* I.57: "indeed in no other way was it possible for us to possess from childhood such a number of important ideas, innate and as it were impressed on our souls . . . unless the soul, before it entered the body, had been active in acquiring knowledge." *On Laws* I.33: "we are so constituted by Nature as to share the sense of Justice with one another and to pass it on to all men. And in this whole discussion I want it understood that what I shall call Nature is [that which is implanted in us by Nature]." See also *Tusc.* III.2; *On the Greatest Good* V.18.
35. See Plato *Meno* 82a–85e; Cicero *Tusc.* I.57.
36. See Plato *Apology* 22a–c; *Phaedrus* 245a; *Ion* 533d–534e; *Laws* 719c–d: "when a poet takes his seat on the Muse's tripod, his judgment takes leave of him. He is like a fountain which gives free course to the rush of its waters." Cicero *On Divination* I.80: "And poetic inspiration also proves that there is a divine power within the human soul. Democritus says that no one can be a great poet without being in a state of frenzy, and Plato says the same thing. . . . And what about your own speeches in law suits? Can the delivery of you lawyers be impassioned, weighty, and fluent unless your soul is deeply stirred?" *In Defense of Archias* 18: "And yet we have it on the highest and most learned authority that while other arts

[14] Thus you must accept that if the spirit is not prevented by passions and perverse attitudes, it would undoubtedly dedicate itself to the study of wisdom and learn, in a short time and fitting manner, the total accumulation of knowledge that has been discovered and passed on by the most distinguished scholars. If, on the contrary, the mind has applied itself but still has not advanced at all or only very little, then either the mind lacked a sufficient number of teachers or its well-disposed nature has been hindered by the incompetency of the teachers. But, then, if there were a sufficiency of educators whose instruction had been suitable, and yet the mind had not appropriated the whole world of arts and sciences, it must then mean that it had approached the arts and sciences with some other motivation. The mind may have applied itself to one discipline for profit, to another for enjoyment, and to a third for ostentation. For you, however, during this most fortunate period, there is at hand an abundance of professors of whom none were ever wiser or more learned. Here they are seated in their honorable ranks willing to guide you. They will present and explain in a clear fashion, with a well-organized method and an unbiased presentation, those disciplines that they have mastered during long, sleepless nights by hard work and sweat. This group of masters of great authority, which they exercise with incredible prudence and wisdom, and which is the reward of their

---

are matters of science and formula and technique, poetry depends solely upon an inborn faculty, is evoked by a purely mental activity, and is infused with a strange supernal inspiration. Rightly, then, did our great Ennius call poets 'holy,' for they seem recommended to us by the benign bestowal of God." *On the Orator* II.194: "For I have often heard that . . . no man can be a good poet who is not on fire with passion, and inspired by something very like frenzy." *Tusc.* I.64: "To my mind even better known and more famous fields of labour do not seem removed from divine influence, or suffer me to think that the poet pours out his solemn, swelling strain without some heavenly inspiration, or that eloquence flows in a copious stream of echoing words and fruitful thoughts without some higher influence." Horace *Art of Poetry* 296–97; Ovid *Treatise on Roman Calendar* VI.5–6: "There is a god within us. It is when he stirs us that our bosom warms; it is his impulse that sows the seeds of inspiration." For similar conceptions and expressions in Cristoforo Landino (1424–98) see *Comento di Cristofaro Landino fiorentino sopra la Comedia di Dante Alighieri poeta fiorentino; impressa in Venetia per Bartholomeo de Zanni da Portese, 1507,* c. 8r, 10–11; in Politian (1454–94) see *Angeli Politiani Sylva, cui titulus Nutricia* in *Opera Omnia . . . (tom.III). Apud Seb. Gryphium, Lugduni 1533,* p. 196 vv. 182–87.

diligent studies, invite you to these same studies so that, according to your own merit, you too can become part of the administration of the state. This splendid age that Charles II, our most powerful king of Spain, has brought about provides an opportunity for you to gather those fruits of peace and tranquillity which have their roots principally in these disciplines. All of our society, which bestows the best positions and responsibility on men of culture, and the entire commonwealth wish that you become most erudite, for they treat such men with honor and praise. All around you are models for you to emulate in your pursuit of the arts and sciences. Incentives abound![37] Inducements are everywhere! A learned faculty is available! A splendid setting is provided! You are born and fashioned to learn to perfection, in a short time and in a fitting manner, the arts and sciences in their fullness! What, therefore, remains? Your will!

37. Vico is inviting these students to important learning, as well as to the possibility of promising and well-paid positions that carry responsibility within the social and political system. He shows an understanding of the changes, social and political, taking place within the society of his time and the surge in power of the new intellectual aristocracy capable of replacing the members of the traditional blood aristocracy. In fact, the Spanish government of Naples had started in 1650 to adopt the criteria of competence and merit in the assignment of public responsibilities and in hiring civil servants from among social groups other than the nobility. The University of Naples, through its courses on juridical and administrative matters, was the agency which prepared such individuals. Vico returns repeatedly to a similar exhortation in the last paragraphs of each oration.

On Virtue and Wisdom

༄རྗེ

Summary of Oration II

The second oration, delivered in 1700, urges that we inform the spirit with the virtues by following the truths of the mind. Its argument is: "That there is no enmity more dire and dangerous than that of the fool against himself." It represents this universe as a great city in which God by an eternal law condemns the foolish to wage against themselves a war thus conceived: "Its law has as many chapters, written out by an omnipotent hand, as there are natures of all things. Let us recite the chapter on man. 'Let man be of mortal body and eternal soul. Let him be born for two things, truth and goodness, that is to say for Me alone. Let his mind distinguish the true from the false. Let not his senses impose upon his mind. Let reason be the principle, guide and lord of his life. Let his desires submit to his reason. . . . Let him win praise for himself by the good arts of his spirit. By virtue and constancy let him attain to human felicity. If anyone foolishly breaks these laws, whether through malice or luxury or sloth or mere imprudence, he is guilty of treason: let him wage war against himself.'" And it proceeds to a tragic description of the war. [*Autobiography*, p. 141]

On Virtue and Wisdom

ORATION II

(Given on October 18, 1700. Argument: "There is no
enemy more dangerous and treacherous to its adversary
than the fool to himself."[1])

[1]   If by any chance one of you could embrace the universe
with the power of his mind, that is, all that is contained in the sky,
the earth, and the sea, he would become aware that all things are
evidence of a sure and correct covenant of harmony. He would also
observe that all these things perform in a unique and equitable
fashion, as they say, the same special functions that were assigned

---

1. This oration develops along Platonic and Stoic lines showing how the fool is
his own greatest enemy. Vico metaphorically describes a war which the fool wages
against himself and about which Giovanni Pico Della Mirandola (1463–94) had
written in *On the Dignity of Man* [trans. Charles Glenn Wallis, Library of Liberal
Arts (Indianapolis: Bobbs-Merrill, 1965), pp. 10–11]: "Indeed, fathers, there is
multiple discord in us, and we have severe, intestine, and more than civil wars at
home: if we are unwilling to have these wars, if we will strive for that peace which
so lifts us up to the heights that we are made to stand among the exalted of the
Lord, moral philosophy alone will still those wars in us, will bring calm successfully. First, if our man will seek a truce with the enemy, he will subdue the
uncurbed forays of the multiple brute, the quarrelings of the lion, and the feeling of
wrath. Then if we take the right counsel, and desire for ourselves the security
of everlasting peace, it will come and will fulfill our prayers liberally. The slaying of
both beasts, like stuck sows, will establish most solemnly a most holy treaty
between the flesh and the spirit. Dialectic will calm the turmoils of a reason shoved
about between the fistfights of oratory and the deceits of the syllogism. Natural
philosophy will calm the strifes and discords of opinion, which shake the unquiet
soul up and down, pull her apart, and mangle her."

to each since the beginning of the world, and that they continue to offer those perennial benefits for which they were naturally constituted.[2] He would undoubtedly affirm that all things have been made according to an eternal model and are ruled by an eternal order. On the contrary, if he would, with the same effort of the mind, concentrate on man, examining him with keenness of mind, he would notice that his interests are not only diverse and contrary, but even foreign and abhorrent to his proper and common nature.[3] He would discover in how many strange and even bewildering ways each man continually changes and, in an hour, would become dissatisfied with himself. He would find that men are lovers of truth but surrounded by errors; they are gifted with reason but subservient to passions; they are admirers of virtue but full of vices; they are searching for happiness but oppressed by miseries; they have a desire for immortality but languish in their idleness of which, as of death, it is best not to speak.[4] I wonder

2. Cicero *Orator* 20–21: "There are in all three oratorical styles, in each of which certain men have been successful, but very few have attained our ideal of being equally successful in all. The orators of the grandiloquent style . . . showed splendid power of thought and majesty of diction; they were forceful, versatile, copious and grave, trained and equipped to arouse and sway emotions; . . . At the other extreme were the orators who were plain, to the point, explaining everything and making every point clear rather than impressive, using a refined, concise style stripped of ornament. . . . Between these two there is a mean and I may say tempered style, which uses neither the intellectual appeal of the latter class nor the fiery force of the former; akin to both, excelling in neither, this style keeps the proverbial 'even tenor of its way,' bringing nothing except ease and uniformity."

3. See Lucretius *On the Nature of Things* III.1053–70: "Even as men evidently feel that there is a weight on their minds which wearies with its oppression, if so they could also recognize from what causes it comes, and what makes so great a mountain of misery to lie on their hearts, they would not so live their lives as now we generally see them do, each ignorant what he wants, each seeking always to change his place as if he could drop his burden. There is one goes forth often from his palace who has been bored to death at home, and then suddenly returns because he feels himself no better abroad. Off he courses, driving the nags to his country house [in] headlong haste. . . . Thus each man flees from himself (but of course, as you might expect, the self whom he cannot escape cleaves to him all the more against his will), and hates himself because he is a sick man that knows not the cause of his complaint."

4. Sallust *The War with Catiline* 2.8: "Yet many men, being slaves to appetite and sleep, have passed through life untaught and untrained, like mere wayfarers; in these men we see, contrary to Nature's intent, the body a source of pleasure, the soul a burden. For my own part, I consider the lives and deaths of such men as

that if later he would impetuously hold the irreverent opinion that, because of perpetual collisions and friction of celestial bodies, a certain material, with the potential of bringing forth the human race, fell from heaven.[5] Furthermore, he might be of the opinion that this material was disseminated and planted by good fortune throughout the earth and without any intention has produced man.[6] However, if he would explore this opinion more critically and in more depth, then it would become clear to him how absolutely alien to reason it is and therefore should be disdained and rejected by the minds of all.[7] In fact, how can we suppose on one hand that the inanimate things and those animated but without reason have been made according to an eternal order and are directed by divine Providence, while man alone, on the other hand, who is the most important among all creatures and for whom nature has produced such abundance of useful and pleasurable things, to whom all lands and seas are open for exploration and conquest—that he alone was born by chance and emerged to be tossed by the capricious whim of fortune?[8]

---

about alike, since no record is made of either." See also Seneca *Epistles* 60.4: "Therefore those who, as Sallust puts it, 'hearken to their bellies,' should be numbered among the animals, and not among men; and certain men, indeed, should be numbered, not even among the animals, but among the dead. He really lives who is made use of by many; he really lives who makes use of himself. Those men, however, who creep into a hole and grow torpid are no better off in their homes than if they were in their tombs. Right there on the marble lintel of the house of such a man you may inscribe his name, for he has died before he is dead. Farewell."

5. See Lucretius *On the Nature of Things* I.80–81.

6. Vico alludes to the Stoic doctrine of the origin of man. He is translating almost literally Cicero *On Laws* I.24: "For when the nature of man is examined, the theory is usually advanced (and in all probability it is correct) that through constant changes and revolutions in the heavens, a time came which was suitable for sowing the seed of the human race." See also Terence *The Eunuch* 134.

7. Cicero *On Fate* 47: "This is wishful thinking, not investigation. For you do not say that the atom moves its position and swerves owing to being driven by an external force, nor that there has been any factor in the void through which the atom travels to cause it not to travel in a straight line, nor that any change has taken place in the atom itself to cause it not to retain the natural motion of its own weight. Accordingly although he introduced no cause to occasion this swerve of yours, nevertheless he thinks that he is talking sense when he is saying something that all men's minds scornfully reject."

8. Cicero *On Laws* I.25: "Moreover, virtue exists in man and God alike, but in

[2] If things stand this way, and we nevertheless experience that human nature is without sense, and only in small degree relevant to itself, indeed often rather abhorrent to itself, then it is from here that the ancients, whether they were seers or interpreters of the divine mind, while handing down the sacred rites and mysteries, seem to have spoken something of truth—that we have been born in order to cleanse ourselves of crimes committed by us against ourselves in a prior life. The life that a fool lives is indeed a punishment, the harshest of punishments. Certainly, he is not punished for the crimes mentioned by the poetic theologians, because we could not commit any crime when we did not exist, but rather for acting against that eternal law upon which Almighty God has founded this orderly community throughout the whole world. If all things wish to preserve themselves and, at the same time, save the commonwealth of the universe, while other created things must follow their nature, man instead must follow wisdom as his guide. There are as many chapters of this law written by the omnipotent hand as there are natures and essences of things. We, however, shall recite the one that is relevant for us and was conceived for man: "Let man be made of a mortal body and of an eternal spirit; let him be destined for these two things, truth and goodness, or, indeed, for Me alone; let the mind know the true

---

no other creature besides; virtue, however, is nothing else than Nature perfected and developed to its highest point; therefore there is a likeness between man and God. As this is true, what relationship could be closer or clearer than this one? For this reason, Nature has lavishly yielded such a wealth of things adapted to man's convenience and use that what she produces seems intended as a gift to us, and not brought forth by chance." This is the center and the fulcrum of Oration II. It refers also to another famous text of Pico Della Mirandola on the laws assigned by God to man (*On the Dignity of Man*, pp. 4–5): "We have given to thee, Adam, no fixed seat, no form of thy very own, no gift peculiarly thine, that thou mayest feel as thine own, have as thine own, possess as thine own the seat, the form, the gifts which thou thyself shalt desire. A limited nature in other creatures is confined within the laws written down by Us. In conformity with thy free judgment, in whose hands I have placed thee, thou art confined by no bounds; and thou wilt fix limits of nature for thyself. I have placed thee at the center of the world, that from there thou mayest more conveniently look around and see whatsoever is in the world. Neither heavenly nor earthly, neither mortal nor immortal have We made thee. Thou, like a judge appointed for being honorable, art the molder and maker of thyself; thou mayest sculpt thyself into whatever shape thou dost prefer. Thou canst grow downward into the lower natures which are brutes. Thou canst again grow upward from thy soul's reason into the higher natures which are divine."

from the false and not be dominated by the senses; let reason be the interpreter of life and its guide and overseer; let desire submit to reason. Let mind judge of things not on the basis of opinion, but according to profound reason, and the spirit's quest for the good be according to reason and not passion; let man earn for himself a lasting renown by the good arts of the spirit; let him acquire human happiness by virtue and perseverance. If a fool, whether through malice or luxury or laziness or even by mere imprudence, acts otherwise, let him, guilty of treason, wage war against himself."⁹

[3] Wisdom, therefore, is the law which God has assigned to mankind. We follow nature whenever we direct our minds to the study of wisdom. If, however, we pass from wisdom to folly, then we deviate from our own nature and act against the law whose sanction threatens such immediate and fitting torments that the pain is inflicted by the transgression itself. As the hangman, who puts the chains to the feet, shackles to the wrists, and collar to the neck of the condemned, would not delay in inflicting the torture and then using the hook, so the fool inflicts himself with pain so cruel and rigorous that I dare today to propose it as our very topic: there is no enemy more dangerous and treacherous to its adversary than the fool to himself.

[4] Now I entreat and ask that you will be willing to listen to me attentively and fairly, O privileged youth, who by natural disposition have turned away from folly and have directed your mind to the study of wisdom. I ask this also of you who have made the search for wisdom your professions—you, the highest authorities holding public responsibilities, and you, the most learned doctors of law, committed to learning. I shall try to cover this topic in such a way that its importance along with the brevity of my presentation will compensate for any annoyance provoked by my words and style.

---

9. Cicero *On Laws* II.18–19: "Law is the highest reason, implanted in Nature, which commands what ought to be done and forbids the opposite. This reason, when firmly fixed and fully developed in the human mind, is Law. And so they believe that Law is intelligence, whose natural function it is to command right conduct and forbid wrongdoing."

[5] Certainly I could cite from any epoch of ancient history atrocious and terrible massacres of enemies. But what historical works, annals, or commentaries are there that, scattered on their pages, do not present the readers with many such scenes "O how cruel to tell, how harsh to endure"?[10]

[6] For me to avoid quoting other authors, therefore, I beseech you to form in your own imagination that same savage and terrible vision of battle. After they have called their troops from each camp and have arranged them on the line of battle, the generals give the signal for combat. Then without delay and with shouts exploding from each side, ferocious men rush forward and engage in battle. What hostile and threatening hatred is aroused within their hearts? How great is the unrestrained anger that is unleashed? How much unrelenting furor, companion of audacity, blinds their minds?[11] How much limitless passion for killing invades the spirit? Each with fierce and savage looks threatens the other with a hideous death. Each searches the other with eyes on fire, seeking a vulnerable spot, reaching for it with every thrust of his hand until the deadly iron finally pierces. If some, being driven back, turn to retreat, others press forward. If these hold their line, others attack. Whenever one of the two front lines breaks down, another is formed. When fighting face to face, one kills the other. When they maneuver about the field and pursue each other, they severely wound each other. Many fall, but just as many join in anew. When a few, overcome by exhaustion and wounds, give up, others, fresh and eager, renew the battle.[12] They care for nothing other than slaughter. They strive for nothing other than to wreak destruction. They bring forth nothing but ruin and death. They are determined to maim and murder. When victory has been won, it is possible to see, but not without horror and immeasurable pain, the defeated ones, stricken by panic and in disarray, being executed without

10. Cicero *Tusc.* II.20.
11. Cicero *Concerning His House* 64.
12. Caesar *Civil Wars* III.94.2: "Caesar ordered the third line, which had been undisturbed and up to that time had retained its position, to advance. So, as they had come up fresh and vigorous in place of the exhausted troops, while others were attacking in the rear, the Pompeians could not hold their ground and turned to flight in mass."

mercy while trying to escape. Those who chose to fall where they fought lie alongside the bodies of their enemies, united either by fate or valor, foot soldiers and cavalry, conqueror and conquered, holding in death looks of the rage they held in life.[13] You would see some of the survivors suffocating from the stench and dust; others, in the midst of the massacre, offering their necks to the winner, pleading that he drain away their remaining blood.[14] But the victor humiliates them and makes of them an object of scorn whether for savage pleasure in avenging his own wounds or for the desire of plundering. Without holding back, he slashes the enemy's legs and arms, or even dismembers them that he may the more rapidly rob them of their weapons and shields. Nor is victory final when the battle is over. For presently they turn to devastation of the countryside and pillaging of the cities. Oh! How overcome we are with terror and horror at the sight of those who hide themselves and of those who pull them out of their hiding places; of those who escape and of those who pursue them; of those who resist and of those who trample them down; of the violent among the timid; of the merciless among the miserable; of those who rejoice over the misfortunes of others! Wherever you turn your eye and attention you are surrounded by cruelty and barbarism. The sick one, the old one, the honest woman, the noble virgin, the innocent children, some in their cots, some in the gathering rooms, some in the innermost part of the house, and some in the arms of their parents before altars and family hearths, are deprived of all wealth, dignity, and life itself. All sense of humanity has been silenced. All license to commit the forbidden and the unforbidden prevails.

[7] Indeed, the damage, ruin, and pain inflicted by war seem so overwhelming that even one endowed with a strong and brave spirit would fly from the mere image of such horror and sorrow. However, if one having removed all clouds of error could reach the more resplendent light of truth and could compare the destruction

---

13. Sallust *The War with Catiline* 61.4: "But Catiline was found far in advance of his men amid a heap of slain foemen, still breathing slightly, and showing in his face the indomitable spirit which had animated him when alive."
14. Livy *From the Founding of the City* XXII.51.7.

and pain of battle with that which the fool inflicts upon himself, if sense has any discernment, he would admit that the fool's suffering is far greater. In fact, by pure choice and need we often endure the pain of the surgeon's knife, which may be equal to or perhaps even greater than that inflicted by the enemy on the field of battle. Many who have lost all hope would, if the law did not forbid it, give themselves the same death that the soldier inflicts upon his enemy. Would the enemy deprive us of our homeland? But the hardened criminal, by his own choice and for his own benefit, leaves his territory. Would the enemy take away our riches? But the drunkard and the glutton, immersed in lavish and lascivious deeds, waste their riches. Would the enemy rob us of our freedom? But there are men in desperation ready to sell themselves for whatever gain. On the contrary, (O listeners, your attention! This is of great importance! Take heed! This concerns you directly!), on the contrary, I repeat, the fool declares war against himself, not with the weapons that only wound by piercing or cutting, but with those that inflict the most excruciating torture. He is won by a power beyond which there is none greater. He is deprived of a homeland that is unique. He is robbed of a wealth for which even kings have wished. He is imprisoned in the darkest and harshest of dungeons. He has surrendered himself into a slavery under the most ruthless of tyrants.

[8] You may think that I speak in an exaggerated manner about improbable events. Not so, God help me, not so. I speak about true things, and if there is a fool present, which I doubt, and if he would reflect upon himself, he would confirm from his own experience that I speak the truth.[15] The weapon of the fool is his own unrestrained passion. The power that overcomes him is his

15. Cicero *On the Orator* II.299: "we are told that the famous Athenian Themistocles was endowed with wisdom and genius on a scale quite surpassing belief; and it is said that a certain learned and highly accomplished person went to him and offered to impart to him the science of mnemonics, which was then being introduced for the first time; and that when Themistocles asked what precise result that science was capable of achieving, the professor asserted that it would enable him to remember everything; and Themistocles replied that he would be doing a greater kindness if he taught him to forget what he wanted than if he taught him to remember. Do you observe what mental force and penetration the man possessed, what power and range of intellect?" See also Terence *The Self-Tormentor* 5.74.

conscience. The homeland of which he is deprived is the whole world. The wealth that he loses is human happiness. The dungeon into which he is thrown is his own body. The tyrant to which he surrenders himself is adverse fortune. Please, O listeners, continue to give me your attention and goodwill as you have done while I elaborate each of these themes.

[9] First, consider what terrible enemies and what dangerous weapons the fool prepares against himself. With the same simile found in Philo Judaeus, we may say that there are two powers like a pair of horses in that part of the spirit which is distinct from reason.[16] One is easily provoked to anger, the other easily inclined to lustful desires. The first is male and thus rebellious, spirited, and impetuous; the other female and thus pliable, languid, and idle. The inclination in the former leads toward harsh and difficult tasks while the other embraces light and pleasant things. How many enemies that were hidden come out from those two horses as if each had been a Trojan horse! In fact, when an overwhelming longing for that which has the appearance of good invades the spirit of the fool, love, which is the origin and the source of all passions, is born.[17] If this good is remote, then desire for it is born. If it can be obtained, then hope is built. If it is present, then great joy is aroused. If that good is considered so great and complete that only one man can obtain it, then jealousy and rivalry take over. If one has much of it and we none, then we are consumed by envy. But once we are in possession of what we at first thought as good, its mask now removed, we see its true nature standing forth. What previously had the appearance of good has now disclosed the evil hidden within itself. Then hate, the opposite of love, immediately takes over. If this evil is remote from us, then we despise

16. Philo Judaeus *On Husbandry* 197e–198a.

17. See Cicero *Tusc.* III.24: "the intemperate longing for a supposed great good, and this longing is disobedient to reason, and may be rightly termed desire or lust." Also ibid. IV.12: "Delight and lust on the other hand rest upon belief of prospective good, since lust kindled by temptation is hurried away to the apparent good, and delight shows itself in exuberant transport at having at length secured some coveted object: for by a law of nature all men pursue apparent good and shun its opposite. . . wish is a rational longing for anything. Where, however, wish is alien from reason and is too violently aroused, it is lust or unbridled desire, which is found in all fools."

and fear it. If it is nearby and oppresses us, then we are overcome by distress and misery. At such time the spirit's power, irascible and without delay, may offer a welcome aid to our desperation. Indeed, it causes anger to repel the evil thing for which we formerly longed. If it deems victory possible, then it arms itself with audacity. But if it despairs of victory, then the desire attacks it violently again. If the evil is moderate, the fool is overcome by anxiety. If the evil is very great, the fool is defenseless. Desire and aversion form the front lines of battle against the fool. The next line is exhilaration. On the flanks there is suffering. Besieged by these enemies the spirit of the fool desires, fears, enjoys, and suffers. Because he lacks wisdom, which is the art of living, his desires are not constant, his fears are idle, his spirit's enjoyments are not lasting, and only his apprehensions are enduring.[18] Adolescents wish for perfumes, crowns of flowers, revelries, but at the bottom of these delights they find an emptiness that will infect the rest of their lives.[19] The virile wish for glory, but it is that sought-after glory which dishonored Varro's followers at the defeat of Cannae. Adults wish for power, but impetuous power brought the Sejanuses to the executioner's hook.[20] The old wish for wealth, but such wealth not earned by merit brought Crassus to ruin. The frail wish for long life but must experience the infirmities and troubles of old age as well as witness the funerals of loved ones.[21] The fool has fears, certainly, but his fears have no more substance than those of the child in the dark.[22] The fool is a coward and is like the enemy who abandons its position at the sight of a dust cloud raised by a stampeding herd.[23] For this very reason Seneca quite

18. Virgil *Aeneid* VI.278–79.
19. Lucretius *On the Nature of Things* IV.1131–34.
20. See Juvenal *Satires* 10.66–67.
21. Virgil *Aeneid* IV.617–18.
22. Lucretius *On the Nature of Things* II.57–58: "For even as children tremble and fear all things in blind darkness, so we in the light fear, at times, things that are no whit more to be feared, than what children shiver at in the dark and imagine to be at hand. This terror of the mind, therefore, and this gloom must be dispelled." See also III.89–90, VI.37–38.
23. Seneca *Epistles* 13.8: "consider whether your proofs of future trouble are sure. For it is more often the case that we are troubled by our apprehension, and that we are mocked by that mocker, rumour, which is wont to settle wars, but more

properly and with an excellent euphemism called him a grown-up child.[24] After his infancy but before senility he has nothing more than "a period of childhood, or what is even worse, a childish period."[25] He fears that he will be deprived of the honor due him even in part. But all honor actually depends on those who give it. He fears the loss of his wealth and possessions. But all riches are actually in the hands of fortune. He fears the advancing moment of death. But if even a small drop of blood should block the left ventricle of the heart, death would suddenly arrive.

[10] The joys of the fool (which cannot truly be called joys but rather renewals of pain) are so ephemeral! The fool's enjoyments do not provide continuous contentment but rather a passing diversion. Indeed, that part of the mind empowered with judgment, which has, as it were, been left to the fool for his torment, at times admires men like Archimedes. Even after having defended his country with ingenious implements of war during the sack of Syracuse, he was yet filled with excitement at the sight of the geometric forms made by the ocean on the sands of the beach.[26] It is that part of the spirit which admires men like Scipio, who, after having defeated Hannibal and destroyed Carthage, left ungrateful Rome and went to live in his villa at Linternus.[27] There, satisfied by his accomplishments and with his spirit at complete peace, he dedicated himself to the study of letters. He delighted himself both in the pursuit of wisdom and in the recollection of his past glories. Virtue is for itself so attractive that even immoral persons are naturally inclined to approve that which is the best. What then?

---

often settles individuals. Yes, my dear Lucilius; we agree too quickly with what people say. We do not put to the test those things which cause our fear; we do not examine into them; we blench and retreat just like soldiers who are forced to abandon their camp because of a dust-cloud raised by stampeding cattle, or are thrown into a panic by the spreading of some unauthenticated rumour."

24. Ibid. 24.13.

25. Ibid. 4.2: "You remember, of course, what joy you felt when you laid aside the garments of boyhood and donned the man's toga, and were escorted to the forum; nevertheless, you may look for a still greater joy when you have laid aside the mind of boyhood and when wisdom has enrolled you among men. For it is not boyhood that still stays with us, but something worse—boyishness."

26. See Livy *From the Founding of the City* XXV.31.9.

27. See ibid. XXXVIII.53.8; Augustine *City of God* III.21.

The fool suffers that most grave of evils which Persius bequeathed to him with these eloquent words: "Let them see what virtue is and let them be tormented by its rejection."[28] This happens because our reason is moved by the beauty of virtue, for which it has been born, and can hold both affection and passion at bay. But this is not so for the fool. The fool, like Homer's Hector, may be swept away by restless horses. Not knowing the limits of the right, "within which the just can only exist"[29] while he tries to avoid vice he succumbs to its opposite.[30] Contradicting himself, he praises virtue but submits himself to vice. He wishes not to be judged a coward and thus vacillates between timidity and temerity and in the process receives wounds and insults. He wishes not to be judged as one marked by impulsiveness and thus he hesitates before all certainties.[31] He wishes not to be judged as selfish and thus he becomes wasteful of his goods. He wishes not to be judged as squandering and thus he withholds from himself his accumulated wealth as if it were a sacred thing even to the point of depriving himself of necessities.[32] Throughout his life he either burns with desire or shivers from fear. He either becomes consumed with pleasure or is overcome by anxiety. The soul of the fool is besieged by these passions from beneath, by these batterings and assaults. But which force at the end will defeat him? That from which no one is free. It is the remorse issuing from the consciousness of a life of vice. It is this that calls for the Furies and the Erinyes, who will take possession of the fool and vexate him. Would you like to see for yourselves the distress of the fool? Look! The life of the fool is always unpleasant, always fearful.[33] The fool is always in conflict with himself, always hostile to himself. He is remorseful, annoyed with himself, and troubled. He is uncommitted. He changes opinion daily, moving from extreme to extreme. He despises his posses-

---

28. Persius *Satires* 3.38.
29. Horace *Familiar Talks* I.1.107.
30. See ibid. I.2.24.
31. Virgil *Aeneid* IV.298.
32. Terence *Phormio* 44; see also Horace *Familiar Talks* I.1.70–73; Plautus *The Pot of Gold* 724–25.
33. Seneca *Epistles* 15.9: "Here is the proverb; it is an excellent one: 'The fool's life is empty of gratitude and full of fears; its course lies wholly toward the future.'"

sions but at the same time covets those of others. We can speak of him as of Plautus's Alcesimarchus: "his spirit is not where he is, it is where he is not."[34] He is always finding cause for self-condemnation. He is always seeking excitement, never in touch with himself. He is always searching for new surroundings, new responsibilities, new ways of life, initiating new hopes even to the time of death.[35] He is forever fleeing from himself.

[11] Having been assaulted by such weapons, defeated by so great a force, of what most beautiful and great city is the fool deprived? Certainly not the one protected by walls of stone marking boundaries defined by the plow, but rather of the heavenly city encircled by a wall of blazing fire.[36] He is deprived not of a city founded on impermanent laws, but rather of one ruled by eternal law. He is deprived not of a city which venerates its patron deity, but rather of one where the heavens which are the celestial temple of Almighty God open up. As its theater, the world lies open; as its baths, the seas; as its racecourses, the pathways of the sun.[37] Only God and the wise are its citizens.[38] Man's privilege of citizenship is

34. Plautus *The Casket* 211–12.

35. Seneca *Epistles* 13.16: "'The fool, with all his other faults, has this also—he is always getting ready to live.' Reflect, my esteemed Lucilius, what this saying means, and you will see how revolting is the fickleness of men who lay down every day new foundations of life, and begin to build up fresh hopes even at the brink of the grave." See also ibid. 23.9–10, 101.4.

36. Lucretius *On the Nature of Things* I.73: "Therefore the lively power of his mind prevailed, and forth he marched far beyond the flaming walls of the heavens, as he traversed the immeasurable universe in thought and imagination." See also ibid. I.1102, II.1045, 1144, III.16, V.119, 454, 1213.

37. Seneca *Epistles* 90.28: "But wisdom's course is toward the state of happiness; thither she guides us, thither she opens the way for us. She shows us what things are evil and what things are seemingly evil; she strips our minds of vain illusion. She bestows upon us a greatness which is substantial, but she represses the greatness which is inflated, and showy but filled with emptiness; and she does not permit us to be ignorant of the difference between what is great and what is but swollen; nay, she delivers to us the knowledge of the whole of nature and of her own nature. . . . Such are wisdom's rites of initiation, by means of which is unlocked, not a village shrine, but the vast temple of all the gods—the universe itself." See also ibid. 102.21.

38. See Cicero *On the Nature of the Gods* II.154, *On Laws* I.23, *On the Greatest Good* III.64; Seneca *On Leisure* 4.1: "Let us grasp the idea that there are two commonwealths—the one, vast and truly common state, which embraces alike gods and men, in which we look neither to this corner of earth nor to that, but measure the bounds of our citizenship by the path of the sun; the other, the one to

not by birth, nor by one's legitimate children,[39] nor is it a reward earned in the fields of battle or at sea, but only by the possession of wisdom.[40] The law on which this very great community is founded—(pay careful attention to me)—is divine reason, which is present throughout the universe and all its parts. It permeates all things and protects and sustains the world. This divine reason is in God, and it is called Divine Wisdom. It can be known only by him who possesses wisdom, and then it is named human wisdom. What can one with more grandeur and honor say than "I am a citizen of Rome" if not he who can declare "I am a citizen of the universe," which only the wise may do?[41] He is the one who can discern and disclose the truth in all matters above and below, divine and human. Who if not the wise can prove himself fit to be a citizen of this city? It is he who knows and serves the law of nature and the universe. By what means is the law of that commonwealth imparted to both God and man? It is perfect reason by which God acts upon all things and the wise understands all things. What is it that brings man and God together? It is but truth, which only the man of wisdom can comprehend and that abides in God, which Greek makes perfectly clear.[42] What makes man like unto God? It is that virtue which has been exalted by the Stoics. Speaking too highly of the wise and not highly enough of the gods, it was the Stoics who affirmed that it is virtue which molds both the wise and God.[43] The wise is separated from the

---

which we have been assigned by the accident of birth. This will be the commonwealth of the Athenians or of the Carthaginians, or of any other city that belongs, not to all, but to some particular race of men. Some yield service to both commonwealths at the same time—to the greater and to the lesser—some only to the lesser, some only to the greater."

39. Pliny (the Younger) *Panegyrics* 36.3.
40. See Cicero *Tusc.* V.108; *On Laws* I.61.
41. See Cicero *Tusc.* IV.57, V.7; *On Duties* I.153.
42. See *II Epistle of John* 1:1, 2.
43. Seneca *Epistles* 87.19: "Why, then, is the wise man great? Because he has a great soul. Accordingly, it is true that that which falls to the lot even of the most despicable person is not a good. Thus, I should never regard inactivity as a good; for even the tree-frog and the flea possess this quality. Nor should I regard rest and freedom from trouble as a good; for what is more at leisure than a worm? Do you ask what it is that produces the wise man? That which produces a god. You must grant that the wise man has an element of godliness, heavenliness, grandeur. The

celestial beings only by deprivation of an immortality which serves
no purpose for honorable living.[44] Let us affirm this with even
greater devotion, truth, and conviction. It is by virtue alone that
God renders us like unto Himself. It is by virtue alone that He
makes us partakers in happiness with men and in eternal happiness with the celestial beings.

[12] The fool is deprived of a great citizenship. Without doubt
he will lose untold riches and possessions. You may ask: "Lose
what?" Happiness! The expectation of a happy life has been by
nature placed within all mankind. The fool, though wishing for a
life of happiness, flees from it. In a life of happiness there is the
greatest and the truest joy, the greatest and most everlasting peace,
and an unwavering sense of security. The fool, however, has cause
for worry. He travels down a treacherous road which leads him
further away from where he wishes to go. Like those lost within a
labyrinth, the fool becomes increasingly lost by his impulsiveness.[45] Why does this happen? Because he lacks the perfect virtue
which is a harmonious and constant course of life and is acquired
only through the knowledge of things and the practice of wisdom,
both of which prevail in all situations. In truth, the purpose of
human life and the highest of our aspirations is to know the certain and to do the right, to contemplate God by the former and to

---

good does not come to every one, nor does it allow any random person to possess
it." See also ibid. 48.11, 59.14, 73.12–13, 92.30; Cicero *On Laws* I.25.

44. Cicero *On the Nature of the Gods* II.153: "And contemplating the heavenly
bodies the mind arrives at a knowledge of the gods, from which arises piety, with its
comrades justice and the rest of the virtues, the sources of a life of happiness that
vies with and resembles the divine existence and leaves us inferior to the celestial
beings in nothing else save immortality, which is immaterial for happiness."

45. Seneca *Epistles* 44.7: "If there is anything that can make life happy, it is
good on its own merits; for it cannot degenerate into evil. Where, then, lies the
mistake, since all men crave the happy life? It is that they regard the means for
producing happiness as happiness itself, and, while seeking happiness, they are
really fleeing from it. For although the sum and substance of the happy life is
unalloyed freedom from care, and though the secret of such freedom is unshaken
confidence, yet men gather together that which causes worry, and, while travelling
life's treacherous road, not only have burdens to bear, but even draw burdens to
themselves; hence they recede farther and farther from the achievement of that
which they seek, and the more effort they expend, the more they hinder themselves
and are set back. This is what happens when you hurry through a maze; the faster
you go, the worse you are entangled."

imitate Him by the latter. Once we have reached those aspirations we ask for nothing more nor need nothing more. The spirit has completed that for which it was born. When the wise man dedicates himself to this goal, his life is filled with a joy that is accompanied always by tranquillity of conscience and by steadfastness of purity of heart. Through knowledge the wise separates the spirit from the concerns of the body, thus allowing him to devote himself to the better and godlike part. He then can concern himself only when needed with the fragile and troublesome.[46] Thus by inquiring into the nature of all things, by his mind he reaches God and in these meditations he finds delight and sustenance. By having rightly ordered his life he is aware that there are within us both desire and aversion, both virtue and vice, while on the outside of us there are the body, riches, and glories.[47] He knows that what is within us is by its nature free and serves him only, but what is on the outside is subservient and under an alien law. Therefore, he conducts himself in such a manner as to accept with equanimity of spirit whatever the decree of God demands that he endure. He knows that he is bound by this oath—to bear all mortal conditions and to be unperturbed by those which are not possible to escape.[48] And so from the fortress on the highest summit of his mind, he can look down on the dominion of fortune and, as from the highest peak of Mount Olympus, resist all winds and storm clouds of human affairs.

[13] The fool is deprived both of these many and great possessions and also of his freedom, I say, by right of a just war. Not the freedom bestowed upon the slave by his master with the staff of manumission or the skullcap, but the freedom bestowed by the authority of wisdom. The fool, deprived of his freedom, is confined in a dungeon of impenetrable darkness and surrounded by terrifying things. In this dungeon not the slightest cleft is open through which the thinnest ray of light can pass. No truthful superintendent presides here, and the deceitful guard of the dungeon delights in giving false reports from the world outside.

46. See ibid. 78.10.
47. Ibid. 124.3.
48. See ibid. 76.23.

[14]   I believe that by now you have understood well what I am saying. The dark dungeon is our body. The wardens are opinion, falsity, and error. The guards are the senses, which are the keenest in childhood but dulled by old age and throughout life severely impaired by perverse passions. A disease of the nerves, a defect of the organs, or an intemperate desire will alter and reduce their power. What? Diverse bodily structures cover many different and even contrary natures? In how many ways does love distort our judgment? In how many ways does hate impede it? He who loves praises the deficiencies of his beloved as if they were virtues. He who burns with hatred sees her good qualities as if they were abhorrent.[49] Man is tossed by unending waves of conjecture. He is overpowered in the narrow straits of passions. He flounders against the rocks of error. Because he lacks wisdom as his pilot, the fool surrenders himself into the hands of fortune. Because he knows not the reason of things, he is ignorant both of what to do and what not to do.[50] Buffeted by the raging whims of fortune, he cries out from the affliction of his spirit—"I am undone! Hope has failed me! I could not have known this would be my reward!"[51]

[15]   O Plato, soul and pupil of the eye of all the wise, how truly and well you have said that the man who is a fool is among animals the most ferocious![52] Is there indeed a greater ferocity, or better still let us call it savagery, than to wage that unnatural war against oneself? Is there indeed a greater savagery than to submit oneself by conscience to the yoke of shame hour after hour? Is there indeed a greater savagery than to have no citizenship in such

49. See Lucretius *On the Nature of Things* IV.1153–70; Cicero *On the Nature of the Gods* I.79; Horace *Familiar Talks* I.3.38–40.
50. See Lucretius *On the Nature of Things* I.75–77, V.89–90, VI.64–66.
51. See Cicero *On Duties* I.81: "Now all this requires great personal courage; but it calls also for great intellectual ability by reflection to anticipate the future, to discover some time in advance what may happen whether for good or for ill, and what must be done in any possible event, and never to be reduced to having to say 'I had not thought of that.' These are the activities that mark a spirit strong, high, and self-reliant in its prudence and wisdom." Also Seneca *Epistles* 76.35: "Hence, the wise man accustoms himself to coming trouble, lightening by long reflection the evils which others lighten by long endurance. We sometimes hear the inexperienced say: 'I knew that this was in store for me.' But the wise man knows that all things are in store for him. Whatever happens, he says: 'I knew it.'"
52. Plato *Laws* 765e–766a.

an excellent city? Is there indeed a greater savagery than to be deprived of the riches which are ours? Is there indeed a greater savagery than to be cast into that dungeon from which there is no escape? Is there indeed a greater savagery than to remain in the clutches of that cruelest mistress and not take refuge in the sanctuary of wisdom? Come, then, finally, let us consider ourselves! Let us be merciful to ourselves! Let us make a sacred covenant with ourselves! The Fetiales are here to witness this covenant. They will even give us the solemn words. Let us repeat after them.[53] Let us obey that law of nature which commands each of us to be true to himself. It is within our power because it is indeed within us. It is for our well-being because it is indeed within nature.

53. See Cicero *On Laws* II.21: "Your admission leads us to this: that animal which we call man, endowed with foresight and quick intelligence, complex, keen, possessing memory, full of reason and prudence, has been given a certain distinguished status by the supreme God . . . ; for he is the only one among so many different kinds and varieties of living beings who has a share in reason and thought, while all the rest are deprived of it. But what is more divine, I will not say in man only, but in all heaven and earth, than reason? And reason, when it is full grown and perfected, is rightly called wisdom. Therefore, since there is nothing better than reason, and since it exists both in man and God, the first common possession of man and God is reason. But those who have reason in common must also have right reason in common. And since right reason is Law, we must believe that men have Law also in common with the gods. Further, those who share Law must also share Justice; and those who share these are to be regarded as members of the same commonwealth."

On True Learning

❧❀❧

Summary of Oration III

The third oration, delivered in the year 1701, is a kind of practical appendix to the two preceding ones. Its argument is: "That the society of letters must be rid of every deceit, if you would study to be adorned with true not feigned, solid not empty, erudition." It points out that in the republic of letters one must live justly; it condemns the wilful critics who wrongfully exact tribute from this public treasury of letters, the stubborn sectarians who keep it from growing, and the impostors who counterfeit their contributions to it. [*Autobiography*, pp. 141–42]

On True Learning

⋎ৡৎ⋏

ORATION III

(Given on October 18, 1701. Argument: "If we would
study to manifest true, not feigned, and solid, not empty
erudition, the Republic of Letters must be rid of every
deceit.")

[1]   Of all the great gifts of Almighty God which are as numerous as all things that have come from the darkness of nothingness
into the light of the world, none is more splendid and magnificent
a gift given to the human mind, if you would rightly reflect upon
this, as the free will which originated from His infinite goodness.
It is a most wondrous gift, indeed even one appropriate to royalty
that man alone may command, while all other created things, by
their nature, must serve. The earth stands eternally balanced in its
mass without faltering or wavering.[1] The ocean without interrup-
tion is stirred up by its surging but never goes beyond its shores.

1. Cicero *Tusc.* V 69: "With what joy, pray, must then the soul of the wise man
be thrilled when in such company he spends his life and passes his nights in their
study! When for instance, he discovers the movements and revolutions of the whole
heaven and sees the countless stars fixed in the sky in unison with the movement of
the vault itself as they keep their appointed place, . . . no wonder the spectacle of
all this stimulated those men of old and encouraged them to further search. Hence
sprang the investigation into the beginnings and as it were the seeds from which all
things got their origin, propagation and growth, to find out what was the beginning
of each kind whether inanimate or animate, or mute or speaking, what life is, what
death, and what the change and transmutation from one thing into another, what
the origin of the earth."

The sun accomplishes its daily and annual movements without losing a bit of power or stopping even for an instant. At one appointed time the year grows green, and at another it produces the harvest. The lion never becomes meek, nor does the hare acquire great courage.[2] While the tiger holds its ferocious nature, the cow maintains her gentle one. Man alone is whatever he chooses to be. He becomes whatever he desires to become. He does whatever pleases him.[3] After Adam, first of mankind, was created by God out of the noble Syrian clay,[4] I believe that the entirety of things which is the world, if it had any awareness, would see man alone to be the director of his own actions while all other created things are nature's slaves. Because of his freedom, which no other created thing possesses, the world would recognize him as being, if not its lord, then nearly its lord.[5]

[2] O would that God Eternal had made man subservient to his own nature like all other creatures! With his will thus shackled, man would then follow the course of right reason for which he was intended. He would strive to achieve his goals in a manner of even greater consistency than that of the sun and stars tracing out their course. He would maintain a constancy in life more stable than that of the earth itself. He would maintain himself within the

2. See Seneca *Epistles* 85.8: "Again it makes no difference how great the passion is; no matter what its size may be, it knows no obedience, and does not welcome advice. Just as no animal, whether wild or tamed and gentle, obeys reason, since nature made it deaf to advice; so the passions do not follow or listen, however slight they are. Tigers and lions never put off their wildness; they sometimes moderate it, and then, when you are least prepared, their softened fierceness is roused to madness. Vices are never genuinely tamed. Again, if reason prevails, the passions will not even get a start; but if they get under way against the will of reason, they will maintain themselves against the will of reason. For it is easier to stop them in the beginning than to control them when they gather force."

3. See Giovanni Pico Della Mirandola *On the Dignity of Man* [trans. Charles Glenn Wallis, Library of Liberal Arts (Indianapolis: Bobbs-Merrill, 1965), p. 5]: "It is given him to have that which he chooses and to be that which he wills."

4. Vico may have derived this information from the work of Gabriel Sionita and Ioannes Hefronita Maronita (seventeenth century), *De Nonnullis Orientalium Urbibus nec non . . . Amsterdami apud Guilielmum et Ioannem Blaeu, 1635* (chap. 4, pp. 18–19), in which Damascus, *in qua Adam formatus est* (in which Adam was created), is described as a city and the meaning of its name is explained. The tradition that recognizes the city of Damascus with its gardens and fountains as the earthly paradise is present in the *Qur'an* Sura XVII.1 and XXIII.52.

5. See Marsilio Ficino *Platonic Theology* XII.3.

limits dictated by human and divine law more devotedly than the ocean confines itself within its shores. He would reap the right and appropriate harvest of virtue for each period of life. Throughout his life, he would show forth examples of justice. In adolescence those would be examples of temperance; when an adult, those of fortitude; and when he is advanced in years, those of prudence. He would never for pleasure abandon his human nature and be transformed by some Circean potion into a brute animal intent on its own gratification.[6] Indeed, the freedom of choice of the human spirit is the reason for all evil. All misfortunes, all ruin, all plagues of mankind are derived from it. Man, by the abuse of his freedom of choice, has made harmful all things that were previously inoffensive to his nature. He has built above him a great wall of stone, but it will crush him. He has dared to entrust himself to the sea, but it will shipwreck him. He has sharpened the iron, but it will inflict wounds upon him. The pleasures of the palate count far more than the needs of the body. With wine he has subverted sleep. He brings upon himself his own destruction by sumptuous feasting. From all directions he has raked together those forces that will corrupt and destroy his nature.[7]

[3]   These afflictions, however, are more tolerable than those brought about by one who misuses the literary studies. It is these studies that are intended primarily for overcoming the harm brought about by the corrupted free will. Thus the one who misuses these studies would change that which is the sustenance and pleasure of the spirit into a detestable and deadly venom. By his evil will he would infect, as with a contagion, these very studies that are intended, either alone or with other disciplines, to bring about a peace to the spirit and to instruct in the most worthwhile manners of society. But, on the contrary, they will turn out to be a source of anxiety and care. As Epictetus has said, one man may show forth a pretended knowledge, while another possesses a vain

6. Cicero *On Divination against Caecilius* 57.
7. Sallust *The War with Jugurtha* 89.7: "the Numidians lived for the most part on milk and game, making no use of salt and other whets to the appetite; for in their opinion the purpose of food was to relieve hunger and thirst, not to minister to caprice and luxury." See also *The War with Catiline* 13.3.

knowledge.[8] The first wishes to be seen as a learned man though he is not. The second, though he is unquestionably learned, has brought together all his learning, not for the purpose of achieving wisdom, nor an unassuming conduct, nor a gentleness of spirit, but for a pointless ostentation.[9] Lest you fall into either of these errors, O youth of greatest promise who are striving for your place in the community of the truly learned and wise, do this day take this solemn oath: that you spurn from your studies, to the best of your ability, all intentional deception. This is the principal theme of what I wish to say. Come! Follow along with me!

[4] Indeed, there is such a great and powerful force inherent in the soul of man which leads him to associate and join together with others, that no person, however wicked or treacherous or wretched, can be found to exist without it. There is none, though he be so depraved, who does not hold and nurture some sense of the just like a glowing cinder concealed by the ashes.[10] In witness to this, even pirates and thieves, although untrustworthy in all other situations, observe the rules of their clandestine societies with a nearly religious fervor, together facing common dangers with manliness, coming to each other's aid in times of threat, and dividing their spoils in good faith among themselves.[11] Concern-

8. See Arrian *Discourses of Epictetus* II.19.12–17; Gellius *The Attic Nights* I.2.6.

9. This expression is a literal copy of an analogous phrase of Tommaso Cornelio (1614–84), in *Thomae Cornelii Consentini Progymnasmata Physica . . . Neapoli 1688, ex typographia Iacobi Raillard*, p. 91. Together with Leonardo Di Capua (1617–95), Tommaso was a pioneer of the new scientific awakening which prospered during Vico's youth. See *Autobiography*, pp. 33, 133, 147.

10. Cicero *On Duties* II.39–40: "Now, in my opinion at least, every walk and vocation in life calls for human co-operation—first and above all, in order that one may have friends with whom to enjoy social intercourse. And this is not easy, unless one is looked upon as a good man. . . . So also to buyers and sellers, to employers and employed, and to those who are engaged in commercial dealings generally, justice is indispensable for the conduct of business. Its importance is so great, that not even those who live by wickedness and crime can get on without some small element of justice. For if a robber takes anything by force or by fraud from another member of the gang, he loses his standing even in a band of robbers."

11. See Plato *Republic* I.351.c–d; Cicero *On Duties* II.40. Similar ideas are found in Juan Luis Vives (1492–1540), *De Tradendis Disciplinis*, V. Vives also recommends that scholars should relate the one to the others with honesty and respect in order to create a 'saintly' association, whose members would care for the advancement of learning and not for financial profit or personal glory. [This work

ing those men who have happened into the community of letters either with a pretended knowledge or a vain learning, observe and judge how solemnly they uphold and practice the laws of that society. Examine those laws and judge for yourselves how they are obeyed.

[5] For all associations of men this is the intended law: that each member bring with him to share in common either his goods or his talents. As reason unites men, language nations, government citizens, name families, blood kin, and commodities merchants, it is necessary both that scholarship should bring together professors of liberal arts and that the inquiry into the nature of all things unite philosophers. Is the rhetorician abiding by this law or disregarding it when he contributes nothing of his own to the academic pursuits but rather, with the teeth of Theon, tears apart and destroys the efforts of others?[12] Does he abide by this law when he discounts Virgil from among the heroic poets because the judicious Longinus compares Cicero with Demosthenes without mentioning Virgil with Homer?[13] When together with Asinius he tears apart Cicero, the tongue, marrow, and heart of eloquence, as disorganized and fragmented, and together with Cato ridicules him?[14] When he says that the gods of Plautus act like parasites and that the slaves of Terence philosophize? When he comments that Livy is as verbose as Caligula? When with the same Pollio Asinius he reprimands Sallust for affectation in using words of false antique coinage? When he criticizes the style of Ovid as ambitious and artificial to the point of fastidiousness? When he detests the swelling style of Lucan? When he derides Martial as a fool to be scorned in the public square?[15] Is the philosopher abiding by this

is available in English: *Vives: On Education*, trans. Foster Watson (Totowa, N.J.: Rowman and Littlefield, 1971).—*Trans.*]

12. Horace *Epistles* I.18.81–82.

13. See Pseudo-Longinus *On the Sublime* 12.4.

14. See Plutarch *Cato m.* 21.7–8. *Cicero synk.* 5. Not Asinius but M. Junius Brutus criticized Cicero and considered him to be disorganized and disconnected, *elumbis*, and fragmented, *fractus*. It is, however, true that both Pollio Asinius and Gallus Asinius, his son, had no appreciation for Cicero's oratorical art.

15. For this evaluation of classic authors see Suetonius *Caligula* 34.2; *On the Grammarians* 10; and also Gellius *The Attic Nights* X.26.1. In Plautus's *Amphitryon*, after having assumed the mortal traits of Sosia, Mercury acknowledges

law or disregarding it when he contributes nothing of his own to the common store of knowledge but rather degrades the contributions of others? When he charges Plato with being an author of legends for old women? When he accuses Zeno of being a false prophet of wonderful things, boastful, arrogant, and full of pride?[16] When he denigrates Democritus and Epicurus as men interested only in carnal pleasures? When he calls Descartes a poetaster of nature? When he shamelessly collects all of the most slanderous epithets against Aristotle that have been heard coming from "the fools, the ignorant, the simpletons, the dolts, the stupid ones, the feebleminded, and the babblers?"[17] Is the physician

---

being Jupiter's parasite (verses 515, 521, and 993). In Terence's *Lady of Andros* a different Sosia speaks using philosophical expressions. From this, the accusation is derived that the gods of Plautus behave like parasites and that the slaves and servants in Terence talk like philosophers. The first objection to Ovid's art is found in Marcus Annaeus Seneca *Controversial Topics*, II.10.4: "in his poems . . . he did not ignore but rather he loved his own vices," and in IV.28.5: "Ovid does not know when it would be better to give up." Vico may have been influenced by Daniel Crispinus Helvetius's edition of Ovid's *Opera* (Lugduni, 1689), in which he could read: "he would prefer to limit the rich and triumphant style of Naso instead than to add . . . those so much praised qualities of Naso's genius, because even though so great they however are not such that they greatly shine forth and therefore be approved by me" (1:3–4). Criticizing Lucan and his admirers, Iulius Caesar Scaliger (1484–1558) writes such phrases as this: "Therefore, as much as I am free to say, Lucan seems to me to bark and certainly not to sing," in *Iuli Caesaris Scaligeri, viri clarissimi, Poetices Libri Septem: I historicus, . . . VI hypercriticus . . . Apud Ioannem Orispinum, n.l. (sed Lugduni) 1561*, p. 325.

16. See Cicero *On the Greatest Good* III.5: "Philosophy is the Science of Life, and cannot treat its subject in language taken from the street. Still of all the philosophers the Stoics have been the greatest innovators in this respect, and Zeno their founder was rather an inventor of new terms than a discoverer of new ideas." *Tusc.* V.34: "And if Zeno of Citium, a mere foreigner and an obscure coiner of phrases, seems to have wormed his way into ancient philosophy, let the full weight of this opinion be obtained afresh from the authority of Plato, in whose pages we often find the expression used that nothing should be called good except virtue." Descartes (1596–1650), in his reply to the fifth set of objections by Pierre Gassendi (1592–1655), makes continuous use of the word *carneus*, specifically referring to Epicurus, "a man made only of flesh," and addresses himself to Epicurus with the vocative "O flesh!" [*Descartes, Selections*, ed. by Ralph M. Eaton (New York: Scribner's, 1955), pp. 250ff.]. Cicero *On Duties* III. 39.

17. Plautus *The Two Bacchises* 1057. Vico uses this verse of Plautus to disapprove of the criticism made by Leonardo Di Capua in his *Ragionamenti intorno alla incertezza de' medicamenti, Ragionamento Ottavo*. Di Capua repeats the criticism of Lactanctius, Jerome, Ambrose, and Tertullian against Aristotle. Vico corrects Di Capua by affirming that he violates the solidarity that must unite all scholars when he attacks Aristotle without acknowledging that in Aristotle which is valid and important.

abiding by this law or disregarding it when he contributes nothing of his own to the common well-being but rather dissects away the medicine of the ancients from that of today? Is the jurisconsult abiding by this law when he judges Accursius a barbarian ignorant of all things or testifies that the followers of Jacques Cujas have knowledge of nothing else than the formalities of the law regarding emancipations and the contracts written according to the regulations of the brass and scales?[18] Are all of these associations in the interest of personal gain without suffering personal discomfort?[19] O youth, scion of the best families, sweat, exhaust your energies, work through the nights, record your readings, accept challenges! Whatever the envious say of others, they will say it also of each one of you. Apply yourselves and persist! In your studies of rhetoric avoid the errors of others not by insulting them but by writing with your best efforts. In your studies of philosophy challenge the errors and the fallacies of others not with insults and abuses but with reasons and arguments that are to the point.

[6] The nature of society is, indeed, founded on mutual good faith. Thus the ancients in matters regarding society have put forth in writing that rule of law: "Among the good behave well."[20] The strength and the authority of this is such that as a duty it acquires the force of law. O Eternal God! If in societies that are based on profit making the members act equitably and fairly with one an-

18. Vico alludes to Lorenzo Valla's (1407–57) criticism in *Laurentii Vallae Elegantiarum Latinae linguae libri sex nec non in Bartoli de 'insigniis'. . . in Opera . . . Basileae, apud Henrichum Petrum, mense Augusto, anno 1543,* p. 633, of Franciscus Accursius (1182–1253), a jurist, whom, on the contrary, he greatly admired. Jacques Cujas (1522–90) and his disciples worked on the exegesis of the juridic text concerning inheritance. The expression of a *testamentum per aes et libram* refers to a specific ritual involved in making up a legal testament.
19. See Ulpian *Digest: For a Partner* XVII.2.29.2, 52.4.56.
20. Cicero *To His Friends* VII.12.2: "But how on earth will you uphold the principles of civil law, when your every act is for yourself alone and not for your fellow-citizens? Besides, what will become of the legal formula in cases of trust, that *dealings between honest men should be in accordance with honesty?* For who is an honest man, who does nothing except what is his own interest? What would be your legal ruling as to dividing what is held in common, when nothing can be held in common among those whose one standard of conduct is their own pleasure?" *On Duties* III.61.70: "pretence and concealment should be done away with in all departments of our daily life. Then an honest man will not be guilty of either pretence or concealment in order to buy or to sell to better advantage. . . . In a suit for the restoration of a trust: 'honest dealing, as between honest parties.'"

other, will the members in the scholarly societies act unfairly with each other? Restrain yourselves from this vice, O youth! Praise the authors for that in them which is to be admired. But for that in which they fail, attribute it to human frailty and have compassion for the shortcomings of our common human nature. Therefore, O youthful rhetoricians of admirable qualities, honor Plautus for his Latin, find delight for yourselves in the elegant style of Terence, and praise the exalted majesty of Virgil. Praise the stream of eloquence of Cicero[21] which flows with boundless abundance as overflowing and as inundating as Virgil's shepherd saw issuing forth from the rock.[22] Accept the plentiful milk of Livy along with the sour fury of Sallust.[23] Collect the colorful flowers of Ovid. Admire the bold endeavors of Lucan. Applaud the wise sayings of Martial. If you have dedicated yourselves to philosophy, listen then to Plato as he considers the immortality of spirit, the eternal and inexhaustible power of divine ideas, of Genii, of God, who is the Supreme Good, and of love free from passion. You would then know why he has rightly merited the name of Divine. Listen to the Stoics, how seriously and authoritatively they teach about the steadfastness of the wise. You would surely recognize them as the rigid and stern custodians of virtue. Listen to Aristotle and discover with how great a skill he has described the universal human faculty of logical argumentation. After him nothing could be added to logic except further remarks and useful examples. How great is his enthusiasm when he supplies us with instruction in the art of oratory and poetics. Read carefully his most comprehensive system of moral philosophy. You will then proclaim him to be the greatest of minds! Listen to Democritus, how he speculated upon the true similarities in the principles of things, the flow of particles, and the process of sensation. You will then see him as the precur-

---

21. Tacitus *Dialogue on the Orators* 30.5; Quintilian *Rules of Rhetoric* X.1.109.

22. See Virgil *Aeneid*. II.304–8.

23. Quintilian *Rules of Rhetoric* X.1.32: "the famous brevity of Sallust, than which nothing can be more pleasing to the leisured ear of the scholar, is a style to be avoided by the orator . . . on the other hand, the milky fullness of Livy is hardly of a kind to instruct a listener who looks not for beauty of exposition, but for truth and credibility."

sor of the studies of the natural sciences. Listen to Descartes, how he has investigated the motion of bodies, the passions of the spirit, and the means of perfecting vision. Find out how he has meditated on the first philosophy and has applied the method of geometry to the theories of physics. You will discover that he is a philosopher like no other.[24] To you who will be entering the practice of medicine, search Galen and learn with what elegance he assigns names to diseases, with what penetrating ability of mind he detects symptoms, and how many diagnoses he makes with accuracy. You will allow him to be the greatest of physicians.[25] To you who will be entering the profession of jurisprudence, pore over the commentaries of Accursius for yourselves. If the Greek and Latin languages had not been brought back and Roman history reintroduced, I do not believe that we would have known anyone greater in our land than Accursius in the field of jurisprudence. This is what it means to take counsel with the just and the good, to behave well among the good, so that you may have "the capacity of knowing and forgiving."[26]

[7] Therefore, first know and do not judge anyone without a hearing. Who, with knowledge like that of a fair and honest judge, would not balance whatever crime it may be necessary to charge one with by his other deeds done diligently within the law under

24. The *primum verum* is the *cogito ergo sum* ("I think, therefore, I am"). Vico will write extensively on this Cartesian truth in 1710 in *De Antiquissima Italorum Sapientia*. See *On the Most Ancient Wisdom of the Italians Unearthed from the Origins of the Latin Language* [trans. L. M. Palmer (Ithaca: Cornell University Press, 1988)], pp. 53–56, 71–77, 180–85.

25. The scholars who embrace the science of the sixteenth and seventeenth centuries (such as Leonardo Di Capua) not only attacked Aristotle (see note 17 above) but also Claudius Galen (ca. 130–ca. 200). Vico, however, with more prudence, aimed at a continuity with the past by trying to preserve its most valuable discoveries and teachings, discarding what had become obsolete.

26. Terence *The Self-Tormentor* 218–20: "If ever I have a son, I swear he shall find in me an indulgent father, I shall find means not only for discovering but also for pardoning an offence, not like my father who shows me his sentiments under cover of another man. Confound it, when he has a glass or two in him what pranks he relates of his own. Now 'Draw from others,' says he, 'the lesson that may profit yourself.' Cunning old dad! On my word he little knows into what deaf ears he pours his parable." See also *The Eunuch* 42: "So you should recognize facts and pardon new playwrights if they present what their predecessors presented before them."

different circumstances, and then not forgive him?[27] Is it not also true that good faith desires that those same authors, whom you admire by yourselves in the privacy of your homes, you also reward with public praise for their accomplishments?[28] Is it not true as well that good faith desires that the books of others which at home you secretly embrace you should not snub in public?[29] Is it behaving well to give hollow applause after a public reading and then to slight the reader in his absence? Good faith does not tolerate this mockery and detests this kind of backbiting. When you are conscious that an author has written well and has discussed true things, take heed that you do not deceive yourselves in withholding the credit due him. When you are conscious that in some way he has been deceived or has erred or has strayed, do not allow him to persist in his error, but with words well chosen as much as possible, advise him of his faults.[30] The citizens of Athens would vilify with public curses one who gave misleading directions to another who had lost his way, and they would charge him with acting against the nature of human society.[31] Is there anyone who would allow a friend to publish his books which contain obvious falsehood so that later, when no changes can be made, he can persistently harass him about his errors? And is it not the dictate of nature that a man would offer help to another, and yet would a person of letters deny it to a colleague? We must learn, O youth of great hope, in order to know how best to be able to relate

27. See Horace *Familiar Talks* I.3.69–70: "a friend dear to me, as it is right, will he not balance my vices with what there is of good in me?"
28. See Horace *Epistles* I.19.35–36.
29. Horace *Familiar Talks* I.6.5–6; Persius *Satires* 1.118.
30. Cicero *On Duties* I.94, I.18; see Oration I, note 32.
31. Cicero *On Duties* III.55: "for to allow a purchaser to be hasty in closing a deal and through mistaken judgment to incur a very serious loss, if this is not refusing 'to set a man right when he has lost his way' (a crime which at Athens is prohibited on pain of public execration), what is?" I.51: "reason or speech. This, then, is the most comprehensive bond that unites together men as men and all to all; and under it the common right to all things that Nature has produced for the common use of man is to be maintained, with the understanding that, while everything assigned as private property by the statutes and by civil law shall be so held as prescribed by those laws, everything else shall be regarded in the light indicated by the Greek proverb: 'Amongst friends all things in common.'" Horace *Art of Poetry* 404.

humanely to others. Those men (I do not believe that such pests exist in our most noble city!) who suffer through heat and cold in their literary studies, not to be able to help others, but rather only to intimidate them, ought to be exiled to the furthest reaches.[32] They threaten that "He who will have provoked me (I shout aloud—better not to touch me!) will pay for it, and I will defame him throughout the whole city."[33]

[8] Therefore, is one showing good faith, is he acting like an honorable man who is so tied to his beliefs that no possible reason, however powerful, could cause him to give up those beliefs?

"What do you say?"

"The nerves take root in the heart."

"Why so?"

"Because all the ancients unanimously agree in that conviction."

"You've answered well. But if you please, dissect this cadaver."

"Why is there need to pursue this matter since none of us doubts it?"

"Nevertheless, if it doesn't upset you, cut! Indeed, because I'm curious by nature, I'm assaulted by doubt about this matter. Please, cut!"

"None of this is necessary. But just to satisfy you, let's do it!"

"Good! Thank you.[34] Now inspect the heart. What? You stand gazing and turning pale like a superstitious diviner."

"Certainly not."

"Then point out to me the source of the nerves from the heart. You know how very thin the fibers are, don't you? You can't see them. Use the microscope."

"It won't show us very much."

"Nevertheless, use it."

"I'm afraid that my eyes will be injured by such a device."

"There's no danger. We use it every day and there haven't been any injuries."

32. Horace *Art of Poetry* 413; see also Arrian *Discourses of Epictetus* III.15.3.
33. Horace *Familiar Talks* II.1.45–46.
34. Terence *The Self-Tormentor* 360; *The Eunuch* 186; *The Brothers* 946.

"See what you're pushing me into."[35]

"What now? Are you looking at the stock of the nerves in the heart?"

"No, not really."

"Am I right?[36] Didn't I tell you that the nerve filaments are so slender that the eyes aren't capable of seeing them?"

"I hear you."

"Now, listen to me.[37] Look at the brain. Forget the microscope. Observe that on the top of the cerebellum there's a gland called the pineal. Do you see it?"

"Yes."

"Do you also see how the thinnest filaments are directed into the crevices from which all the nerves spread out from the spinal cord to all parts of the body?"

"Yes. I see that as well."

"What now? Aren't you changing your mind?"[38]

"Certainly not. I'm still holding to the opinion which was taught as a child."

[9] In the name of God and man, what is this if it is not removing the sun from the sky in the middle of the day? Please! Purge the stubbornness from your spirit and take on the proper manner of a good man. Hold to an opinion only until another more true is demonstrated. There is no shame in changing your beliefs when erring has been involuntary. Stubbornness is by choice, error by weakness of nature. Please! Do not count yourselves among the number of those contentious men who delight in destructive words which disrupt society—"You say yes, I say no.

35. Terence *The Lady of Andros* 399.
36. Ibid. 423.
37. Terence *The Self-Tormentor* 688.
38. Catullus *Poems* 10.29, 12.4. In order to study medicine it became apparent that it was necessary to learn anatomy. This, however, seems not to have been true for Aristotle and his followers, who also believed that nerves had their roots in the heart without ever having dissected a cadaver. [See Max Harold Fisch, "The Academy of the Investigators," in *Science, Medicine, and History: Essays on the Evolution of Scientific Thought and Medical Practice Written in Honour of Charles Singer*, ed. E. Ashworth Underwood, 2 vols. (London: Oxford University Press, 1953), 1:521–63.—*Trans.*]

You say no, I say yes."³⁹ Please! Be of an open mind throughout your life, and instead choose these words: "I affirm, but it is up to you to make me deny by demonstrating for me a better way."

[10] Finally, good faith excludes all deceit.⁴⁰ If Aquilius has rightly defined it as "to do one thing" and "pretend to do another,"⁴¹ certainly the rhetoricians are pretentious when, after hardly six months or even a year of studying the Greek or Hebrew language, they exclaim like the young native of Attica or Palestine: "Oh if you only knew Hebrew, then you could appreciate the magnificent eloquence of Isaiah! Oh if you knew Greek, then you could savor the sweetness of Plato!"⁴² O eternal God! Ten years is not sufficient to learn the Latin language in order to appreciate fully its elegance and richness, even though today we speak a language derived from it with only a few changes. God knows if any of us has achieved the mastery of it! In fact, can anyone detect the Patavian dialect in Livy or the Gallic in Caesar?⁴³ And in a short time we pretend to know languages totally other than ours, even those no longer spoken! Authors of our times thoroughly acquainted with the Greek and Latin languages claim that Homer,

39. See Terence *The Eunuch* 252.
40. See Paulus Iulius *Digest: For a Partner* XVII.2.3.2.
41. Cicero *Topics* 40; *On Duties* III.60, 61: "When asked what he meant by 'criminal fraud,' as specified in these forms, he [Aquilius] would reply: 'Pretending one thing and practising another'—a very felicitous definition, as one might expect from an expert in making them. Pythius, therefore, and all others who do one thing while they pretend another are faithless, dishonest, and unprincipled scoundrels. No act of theirs can be expedient, when what they do is tainted with so many vices. . . . Pretence and concealment should be done away with in all departments of our daily life." *On the Nature of the Gods* III.74: "hence spring all the trials for breach of trust as to a guardianship, commission, in virtue of partnership, trusteeship, and all the other cases arising from breach of faith in purchase or sale or hire or lease; hence procedure on the public behalf in a private suit . . . ; hence that net to catch wrong-doing of all sorts, the 'action for malicious fraud' promulgated by our friend Gaius Aquilius, a charge of fraud that Aquilius likewise holds to be proved when a man has pretended to do one thing and has done another." Ulpian *Digest: On Bad Faith* IV.3.1.
42. Paulus Iulius *Digest: For a Partner* XVII.2.3.2.
43. Quintilian *Rules of Rhetoric* I.5.56: "I . . . point out that words are either native or foreign. Foreign words, like our population and our institutions, have come to us from practically every nation upon the earth. . . . Pollio reproves Livy for his lapses into the dialect of Padua." Ibid. VIII.1.3.

compared to the example of Virgil, is sordid and inept, Demosthenes, compared with Cicero, is stale and frigid. Ah, listeners! To quote Sallust, we carry our faults into our occupations.[44] Homer is not sordid, nor Demosthenes stale. It is we who do one thing and pretend to do another. It is our ignorance of this language that does not permit us to know how great is the weight of the function of its words, the elegance of its expression, the resonance of its sound. Since the time when the Greek language flourished and the Greeks and Romans were integrated over a long and productive period, Virgil dedicated himself to the one goal that Rome should have its own Homer and Cicero concentrated all of his efforts so that Latium could have its Demosthenes. Do we, now that the Greek language has become utterly extinct, dare to pronounce those judgments upon Homer and Demosthenes? Concerning the Hebrew language, I will briefly explain what place it holds in the judgment of the experts and of those who use it most. In the Hebrew language we have only the sacred books of the Old Testament. A grammar of Hebrew was formulated about a thousand years after Christ. But these grammars were based either on ancient versions, or the authority of the Massoretes, or the rabbis. Of these ancient versions, the one which is best known to us is the Vulgate, which the ages have confirmed to be changeless throughout the centuries of the church. Judge for yourselves the condition of the text of all the other ancient versions from what we say of the oldest among them, that called the Septuagint. It was compiled

44. Sallust *The War with Jugurtha* 1.3–4: "But the leader and ruler of man's life is the mind, and when this advances to glory by the path of virtue, it has power and potency in abundance, as well as fame; and it needs not fortune, since fortune can neither give to any man honesty, diligence, and other good qualities, nor can she take them away. But if through the lure of base desires the mind has sunk into sloth and the pleasures of the body, when it has enjoyed ruinous indulgence for a season, when strength, time, and talents have been wasted through indolence, the weakness of human nature is accused, and *the guilty shift their blame to circumstances.*"
Iulius Caesar Scaliger, *Poetry Books*, V, maintained the superiority of Virgil over Homer. The origin of the judgment given by those who supported the superiority of Cicero over Demosthenes seems to be in Petrarch (1304–74) *On the Ignorance of Himself* IV.13 and in *Fame Triumphing* III.18–24. Most humanists followed Petrarch as did Tommaso Campanella (1538–1639) in *Thomae Campanellae De libris propriis et recta ratione studendi . . . , in H. Grotii et aliorum Dissertationes de studiis instituendis. Amstelodami, apud Ludovicum Elzevirium, 1645* (p. 404).

during the reign of Ptolemy Philadelphus, king of Egypt, at least two hundred and fifty years after the return from the Babylonian captivity.[45] By that time, after all the years of slavery in Egypt, the sacred language had become corrupted, and the correct meaning of many words and the purity of the diction had been unavoidably lost. And this is sufficiently apparent from the fact that in numerous passages of the seventy translators one and the same term was rendered in several different ways, so that they agreed among themselves neither about the meaning of the words nor of the subject matter. To this, add the errors of the copyists due either to their negligence or to their ignorance of the language, along with the heretics' art of falsification, and finally the deterioration brought about by time. The Massoretes added the vocalization points at a time when the correct pronunciation of the language was not even known. It will be obvious to anyone who observes the conjectures of the rabbis how weak they were. They tried to confirm the ancient derivation of terms based on the similarity of letters of the alphabet or vocalization points. They concocted inappropriate stories to justify their interpretations. It was, therefore, inevitable that the lexicons compiled in this manner contained numerous errors. I do not make these remarks to discourage you from the most excellent and useful study of this group of languages. Indeed, make every possible effort to master them and to progress to the limits to which our capacities allow us to attain. "It is well to have arrived so far, if it is not permitted to go beyond."[46] But I advise you that we not pretend to know that which in truth we do not know.

[11]   The philosopher acts with deception, doing one thing and pretending to do another, when he disguises his ignorance of things with obviously ambiguous words in order to conceal this ignorance with pretended knowledge.

45. See Augustine *City of God* VIII.11, XVIII.42. The Massoretes (ninth to tenth centuries) and their work were not highly regarded by Vico. See also the *De Uno Opere di G. B. Vico*, ed. Fausto Nicolini (8 vols. in 11) (Bari: Laterza, 1911– 41) 2:179. Vico, too, seems to accept that the Septuagint version was compiled under Ptolemy Philadelphus (309–246 B.C.)
46. Horace *Epistles* I.1.32.

"What's antipathy?"[47]

"It's a certain disposition by which one thing is shown to be incompatible with another."

"For the love of God, explain! Upon what is this disposition founded and based?"

"I'll say in some hidden quality."

"But this is what I ask you. Disclose what this hidden quality is."

He becomes mute and hesitates. Ah, he is about to deceive! Why after admitting his pretension does he not naturally respond at the outset, "I don't know"?

Yet again another philosopher proposes to demonstrate physical phenomena by geometric methods.

"There's nothing I desire more since this is my strong point."

"Then accept these definitions concerning material bodies."

"Yes, I have them."[48]

"Therefore, accept the laws of the motion of these bodies."

"It's a fact."

"Then accept these which I offer as postulates."

"I do."

"From here, using the geometric method, we proceed from what has been investigated and proven indubitable to move step by step in making further deductions."

"Go ahead, I'll follow."[49]

"Don't you see as clearly and plainly as the sum of the angles of a triangle which equals two right angles that bodies fall freely, not by gravity, as they say, but by air pressure?"

"God help me! I don't see it that way!"

"But do you still hold to the premises?"

"Yes, indeed, they are obviously true."

---

47. The writings on "sympathy" and "antipathy" at the time of Vico and before him were abundant. Galen's (second century A.D.) followers maintained the theory that within nature there are similar qualities capable of producing sympathy. There are also dissimilar and uncongenial qualities, which produce antipathy, but they could not explain what these qualities were. Vico criticized them, siding with Leonardo Di Capua.

48. Terence *The Lady of Andros* 86. Vico seems to subscribe to Isaac Newton's (1642–1727) mechanics, rather than to Plato's or Descartes's theories on ether.

49. Terence *The Lady of Andros* 171; *The Eunuch* 908.

"Why, then, don't you agree with me?"

"Because it is possible that some of the rules of Descartes concerning dynamics may be false. Why did I say 'may be' when some of them have been shown to be false by Malebranche?"[50]

Why do we pretend to impose on a man of sane mind geometric demonstrations which he cannot follow? Such a one, although he has unobstructed vision and is vigilant, is still not able to see the sun in full daylight, even though we know that the mind is attracted to truth as the eye is to light. Let us at last confess our natural limitations. Our studies are valuable insofar as we learn that we do not know or we know only a few things.[51]

[12] O rhetorician, you glory in the knowledge of everyday utensils, the dress of the Romans, and you move more freely through the streets, the neighborhoods, and the sections of Rome than through your own city. In what do you feel superior? You know nothing more than does the potter, the baker, the cobbler, the messenger, or the town crier of the Romans. You brag, O philosopher, that you know the principles and causes of things. In what do you brag? Why do you puff yourself up when an adversary can cut you down?

[13] We should, therefore, learn the true value of studies. Let us be aware that the curiosity prohibited our first parent has been punished in us by our being deprived of the true knowledge of things. By this, knowledge separates the educated from the common people. Neither knows. But the common person claims to know, while the educated knows that he does not know.[52] The

---

50. Descartes in the *Principia Philosophiae* (Part II, 46–52) set forth his seven rules on the dynamics of bodies, but Nicholaus de Malebranche (1638–1715) in the *De Inquirenda Veritate* (VI), though recognizing the validity of four of those rules, proved the inaccuracy of three. Vico will repeat this remark once again in 1708 in the *De Nostri Temporis Studiorum Ratione*. [See *On the Study Methods of Our Time*, chap. IV.—Trans.]

51. Vico embraces the Socratic doctrine of *docta ignorantia*, as he was influenced by the humanists and probably by Nicolaus of Cusa (1401–64). Ernst Cassirer explains: "The *docta ignorantia* . . . this concept affirms the idea of knowing ignorance; with relation to experience and empirical knowledge, it affirms the idea of ignorant *knowledge*. Experience contains genuine knowledge; but certainly this knowledge must recognize that, although it may go far, it can only reach a relative aim and end, never an absolute" [*The Individual and the Cosmos in Renaissance Philosophy*, trans. Mario Domandi (Oxford: Basil Blackwell, 1963), p. 23.]

52. Again Vico repeats what Plato's Socrates taught. See *Apology* 21c-d: "in

wise person would speak the truth in all matters if he would affirm all things with only this exception: "I believe this as long as nothing of greater truth stands in its way." Therefore, he would never be deceived or deceive. He would never speak with that voice of the fool: "I believed otherwise." Let us then maintain a society of men of letters from which all deceit has been removed; let us count as gain the abilities of authors; let us balance deficiencies with talents; let us bring something of our own to the common store of knowledge, never professing to have contributed more than we have truly brought. Do you wish for a new way of imitating the virtues of writers? Love their work. Do you wish for a new way to escape their defects? Do not probe with too much eagerness, but should you happen on any defects, treat them with equanimity and benevolence. Do you wish at the same time to be most learned and most honest? Let us strive to be such as we wish to appear.[53] And in this way in the society of men of letters the most abundant fruit that we shall reap is modesty of spirit by which no one would presume to know beyond his measure.[54] And thus, with all deceit overcome, such a one may live his life honestly and sincerely.

---

conversation with him I formed the impression that although in many people's opinion, and especially in his own, he appeared to be wise, in fact he was not. Then when I began to try to show him that he only thought he was wise and was not really so, my efforts were resented both by him and by many of the other people present." Ibid. 23b: "The wisest of you men is he who has realized, like Socrates, that in respect of wisdom he is really worthless." Ibid. 29: "That would indeed be shocking . . . thinking that I am wise when I am not. . . . To think that one knows what one does not know . . . and this ignorance, which thinks that it knows what it does not, must surely be ignorance most culpable." *Hipparchus min. or Lesser Hippias* 372c: "Surely there is a great excuse to be made for a man telling a falsehood or doing an injury or any sort of harm to another, in ignorance. . . . I hope that you will be good to me, and not refuse to heal me, for you will do me a much greater benefit if you cure my soul of ignorance than you would if you were to cure my body of disease." This was accepted by all humanists as one of the cardinal points of their thought.

53. See Cicero *On Duties* II.43: "And yet, as Socrates used to express it so admirably, 'the nearest way to glory—a short cut, as it were—is to strive to be what you wish to be thought to be.' For if anyone thinks that he can win lasting glory by pretence, by empty show, by hypocritical talk and looks, he is very much mistaken. True glory strikes deep root and spreads its branches wide; but all pretences soon fall to the ground like fragile flowers, and nothing counterfeit can be lasting"; and Xenophon *Memorable Things* II.6.39.

54. See Horace *Epistles* I.7.98.

On Education for the Common Good

❧

Summary of Oration IV

The fourth oration, delivered in the year 1704, has this for its argument: "He who would reap from the study of letters the greatest advantages, combined always with honor, let him be educated for the glory and good of the community." It is directed against the false scholars who study for advantage alone and therefore take more pains to seem learned than to be so. When the advantage they seek has been attained, they grow lazy and stoop to the lowest arts to keep up their reputation as scholars. [*Autobiography*, p. 142]

On Education for the Common Good

cᴿ⚘ᴠ

ORATION IV

(Given on October 18, 1704. Argument: "If one wishes
to gain the greatest benefits from the study of the liberal
arts, and these always conjoined with honor, let him be
educated for the good of the republic which is the
common good of the citizenry.")

[1]   If one by chance reflects upon the past two years that have
regrettably interrupted the solemn occasion which, held on this
day, I have faithfully observed for the purpose of exhorting the
youth in the study of the liberal arts, he may wonder why, at this
time, this annual occasion has now been restored to its intent and
custom. He may judge this event as one whose purpose is merely
"a traditional observance" or else "an annual celebration"[1] rather
than as a matter of importance, or he may yet request a further
reason and explanation for our silence.

[2]   It is true that the liberal arts and the sciences are mastered

---

1. Varro *On the Latin Language* VI.61: "*Dico* 'I say' has a Greek origin, that
which the Greeks call *deiknuo* 'I show.' From this moreover comes *dicare* 'to show,
dedicate.' . . . From this *iudicare* 'to judge,' because then *ius* 'right' *dicitur* 'is
spoken'; from this, *iudex* 'judge,' because he *ius dicat* 'speaks the decision' after
receiving the power to do so; from this, *dedicat* 'he dedicates,' that is, he finishes
the matter by *dicendo* 'saying' certain fixed words" Ibid. 95; Cicero *Against Verres*
IV.53. Vico like Varro takes pain to value words and accepts the distinction between the two Latin terms *solennitas* and *solemnitas*. *Solennitas*, which is derived
from *solum* and *annus*, means a yearly celebration; *solemnitas*, derived from *solum*
and *amnis*, indicates a ceremony celebrated near a river.

only with effort. Those who aspire to them will find that they are not easily achieved, not even so readily at hand that one may acquire them while engaging in other activities, nor are they located in such a downward-sloping place that, once enjoyed, their continuing pursuit becomes effortless. On the contrary, so much effort is needed in their attainment that it often seems beyond the limits of human nature. In fact, he who embraces a life of letters must abandon all of his senses completely and totally, which before had been thought to be the most trustworthy guides for living, to see the true nature of things. It is necessary to blind the force that fashions physical images, which is called phantasy, so that he may comprehend the First Truth. It is necessary to expand the narrow limits of the mind and broaden it in order to encompass the boundless realm of nature. Finally, it is necessary to cloud the mind's eye, which is reason, so that the wonders of God, which the Apostle has said to be "beyond demonstration," can be known.[2] And so, all of what I have spoken must be accomplished by adolescents at an age when the vigor of the senses is the greatest, phantasy is the most powerful, the mind is in its most limited state because only now for the first time has it become liberated from the chains of matter, and reason is inquisitive to the point of insolence because it dwells in the total ignorance of things.

[3] If, therefore, by exhortation, admonition, and entreaty, man is persuaded to assume his duties, none of which is foreign to humanity but rather totally in conformity with it, how much more incentive is necessary so that he will surpass his own nature at a time when it is so powerful! Therefore, this exhortation to the study of the liberal arts and sciences has hardly been arranged for ostentation and show. On the contrary, I myself have seen the youth (indeed, every day) who, at such a tender age when they avoid responsibilities and prefer games and sport, after having spent "a long tranquil night"[3] in serious meditation, arrive here at

---

2. Paul, the Apostle *Epistle to the Hebrews* 11:1.

3. Lucretius *On the Nature of Things* I.142: "it is your merit, and the expected delight of pleasant friendship, that persuades me to undergo any labour, and entices me *to spend the tranquil nights in wakefulness*, seeking by what words and what poetry at last I may be able to display clear lights before your mind, whereby you may see into the heart of things hidden."

the crack of dawn drenched to the skin, frozen and shivering from the cold, to listen to their teachers. God help me to force myself according to my ability to exhort them repeatedly every time I see them so that they do not lose courage and give up.

[4]   But if the necessity of this observance is as great as you have perceived, then you will wonder even more why we have interrupted this duty for two years. Indeed, during that time I refrained from giving the orations because there were numerous and compelling events which attracted the eager and motivated youth in their pursuit of wisdom. It was at this time that the most learned men during that entire two years had entered the contest for demonstrating their academic qualifications in order to earn the proposed and prestigious award of being judged fit to teach the youth at public expense. At that same time the most renowned magistrates had been given the authority along with Vincent Vidania, the most venerable and learned dean of studies, to judge the candidates in this contest.[4] They have selected with the greatest competency, profound wisdom, and exceptional perseverance those who will be your future professors. And what, I ask, should interest those as great as these magistrates in your education, O youth of great promise, for such a long time and with such concern? Can it be otherwise than that you are now of special interest to the state so that later you yourselves will wisely show the same concern in the administration of it along with the prince himself? Therefore, if the greatest instigation to the pursuit of civil employment is to be able to enter the service of the state, what should we say when the government itself of its own accord has already committed itself to you? What should we say when it has been preparing you for itself? What should we say when it stands ready in the future to be administered in its various functions by you? Therefore, now that all of those events so numerous and great have quieted down in this university of studies, one which has further

4. Concerning Vincent Diego Vidania (1631–1732), see *Autobiography*, pp. 147, 160–61, 157. Vidania presided over the committee of members who examined Vico in April 1723 when he competed for the chair of civil law. See *Opere di G. B. Vico*, ed. Fausto Nicolini (8 vols. in 11) (Bari: Laterza, 1911–41) 8:289–97.

been enriched by the presence of these most learned teachers, I return to my duty and responsibility. No better argument has occurred to me today which will be more compelling for this exhortation and more appropriate for rendering thanks to the state than the following: "If one of you wishes to gain the greatest benefit from the study of the liberal arts, and these always conjoined with honor, let him be educated for the common good of the citizenry." But before I demonstrate the worth and usefulness of this goal, I judge it to be necessary in a few words, fellow citizens, to account for what necessity binds you together and what degree of love you yourselves share with each other.

[5] You are brothers, O listeners, and you nurture this common civic relationship with true fraternal love. What? You are perplexed? Certainly by your astonishment you accuse me of impudence because I have dared to say that you feel something of which none of you is aware. But neither am I impudent nor are you mistaken in your astonishment. Indeed, the overwhelming number of our kin, as numerous as there are citizens, dilutes and weakens the sense of fraternal love of which I speak. It is decreed by nature that there will be violence in confined places. It is because of this that the sea in narrow straits, even with a soft breeze, can become turbulent, while the open ocean remains tranquil. A river gushes through the gorge but flows with still waters when its bed widens. So also it is with the great love of parents which is spread throughout large families. The more it is distributed among many children the less is given to any single child. But if the hope of offspring is unfulfilled and there remains only one child, on that one who survives, the love toward all who could never be is rekindled and focused. Along the same line, I ask you, think of those who may have left to emigrate to a distant land. Even though they may have acquired friendly and faithful patrons, if by "good chance"[5] one comes upon a fellow countryman, at the mere uttering of the name of their country, they are tied together by a bond of great affection though they are unknown to each other.[6] (At home they may even

5. Terence *The Eunuch* 134.
6. Cicero *On Duties* I.57: "But when with a rational spirit you have surveyed the whole field, there is no social relation among them all more close, none more

have been enemies or hostile toward each other, but here in a foreign land they will very often return friendship the one to the other). Now all of the hospitality and patronage which previously was so important to them is put aside. If you ask the reason for this, either I am mistaken or the bond of fraternal love which they never felt among the multitudes at home now, in their loneliness, they find to be stronger than all other friendships in the new land.

[6] Now you know, O citizens, by what kind of necessity and what degree of love you are united. I am reluctant to spend the time explaining to you who are of such honest and liberal natures what personal advantages there would be for us in being educated for the common good of the citizenry. Therefore, you should learn from other reasons the importance of freely serving the demands and needs of your fellow citizens. In fact, I believe that you can easily understand that the source of this kinship is our homeland. It is the need, affection, and solicitude that we have for our motherland that encompasses the needs, affections and "solicitudes for all others."[7] It is indeed the motherland holding her cloak unfolded before her who cradles devotion to God who will preserve us, loyalty to the sovereign who will guide us, reverence for our forebears who founded our city and established our nation, and grateful memory for our ancestors who have enlarged it and made it illustrious. But by what right better than that we have just given are we attached to our motherland? The motherland has given us birth in this nation which not only is devoted to the true divinity of Almighty God but also glories above all other nations and people of the earth in the supremacy of the religion that was founded in this same land of Italy and has been confirmed over the long course of centuries. It is a gift of the motherland to have been born

---

dear than that which links each one of us with our country. Parents are dear; dear are children, relatives, friends; but one native land embraces all our loves; and who that is true would hesitate to give his life for her, if by his death he could render her service? So much the more execrable are those monsters who have torn their fatherland to pieces with every form of outrage and who are and have been engaged in compassing her utter destruction."

7. [Throughout the passage we have preferred to translate *patria* (one's native land) as "motherland" rather than "fatherland" which is suggested by the root of the Latin term *pater*. We did so because *patria* is a feminine noun and Vico represents it as a feminine figure in this passage.—*Trans.*]

under a sovereign whose empire reaches in all directions so that it would be necessary to create new lands if one would attempt to emulate him in the vastness of his realm. It is a gift of the motherland to have been born in a realm of the empire which has such a good and equitable alliance with its sovereign. I accept as a gift of the motherland that we boast as founders those who came even before the heroic times which man has recorded. They have founded this city in such a congenial place that its inhabitants are born with the greatest ability to learn and are the most talented and robust. They have founded it in soil so fertile and under a sky so benevolent that it is considered to be the pearl of the earth. They have established a society with such just laws and under such favorable auspices that it increasingly profits by lasting virtue and unending happiness. And, at last, it has been propelled forward under the Spanish kings by the multitude and splendor of its public works so that it is now numbered among the most important and prosperous cities in the world. It is another merit of the motherland that we can boast to others of our great forebears, who by the arts of war and peace have given the name of Naples an imperishable glory. The merits of the motherland are so numerous, so great, and so far-reaching that if any of your parents are interested in having you instructed by renowned professors brought from other lands at great expense, it is fitting that your education still be for the benefit of the motherland. It is, in fact, the motherland who has provided your parents with the abundance of wealth which allows them to afford such expenses for your education. And what should we say if one of you with complete self-reliance becomes an educated person on his own, as has been said of Epicurus, without the assistance of any teacher?[8] He still owes this learning to the motherland which has given birth to him so well disposed and with propitious natural talents. What, therefore, should one judge

---

8. See Cicero *On the Nature of the Gods* I.72: "The fact is that you people merely repeat by rote the idle vapourings that Epicurus uttered when half asleep; for, as we read in his writing, he boasted that he had never had a teacher. This I for my part could well believe, even if he did not proclaim it, just as I believe the owner of an ill-built house when he boasts that he did not employ an architect!" Diogenes Laertius *Lives of Eminent Philosophers* X.13; Sextus Empiricus *Against the Mathematicians* I.3.

that each of you owes to the motherland? It is this motherland which has provided you in this university with an abundance of the most learned men in all branches of learning. They offer themselves without expense to you, without inconvenience to you, and without the recommendation of anyone. They have promised to offer their help to you at the expense of the state so that you can be trained in those arts and sciences to which you have been led either by your own inclination or by the advice of your parents.

[7] The laws condemn the thankless freeman who, after having received the greatest benefit of freedom from his owner, and who has expertise in the arts, yet does not come to the aid of his liberator, his children, or his household with those talents.[9] Now how does this relate to him who has received from the motherland not only freedom but the benefits of this great city, his birthright, a well-endowed nature, even his education? Will you, without being called ungrateful, associate with the sons of your homeland who are your brothers for your own selfish reasons? But have I not, without due respect for you, hastened to compare you who are of such creative and free natures with those who were once miserable slaves, and have I not confused the binding of the law with the sense of civic obligation? I will give an example from the most noble citizens of Rome. Rich in years and wisdom, after having served in the offices of consul, augur, priest, praetor, and other important offices in the government, and having thus demonstrated their good judgment in matters both divine and human, they looked forward to an honorable retirement in jurisprudence as though it were a peaceful harbor to their honest lives. They professed, not in their homes or in some other secluded place, but rather while walking "about in the forum" answering questions for those who consulted them.[10] In this way their fellow citizens

---

9. See Ulpian *Digest: On the Right of the Advocate* XXXVII.14.1; Paulus Iulius *Digest: On the Right of the Freeman* XXXVIII.1.16.

10. Cicero *On the Orator* III.132–33: "Do you really suppose . . . that nobody embraced culture as a whole, but instead of that everybody chose for himself a different division to work in? For my part I have often heard my own father and my wife's father say that our people too who desired to win high distinction in philosophy used to embrace all the subjects that at all events at that period were known in our country. . . . We have actually seen Manius Manilius walking across the forum,

would feel not the least hesitation in approaching them in their custom of walking in the forum, nor would any time be wasted since both are going the same way. These wise elders were of the sure opinion that the practical wisdom that they have acquired in the service of the state had to be rendered promptly and clearly for the good of its citizens.

[8] Now consider within yourselves, in the light of the examples I have given, what would be the honest thing for you to do— you who have been educated under the great care of the state, by the wise judgment of the magistrates, by the expertise of the most learned doctors, by the diligent direction of the dean of studies, and at the expense of the public. Allow me now to continue to explore in my lecture what the richest fruits would be that your honest efforts would bear. Certainly if I had spoken to you as men who already possess consummate wisdom, and for whom never is the useful in conflict with the honorable, then having pointed out to you the goal of your studies, I will have proven that this goal is the most useful by having also demonstrated in the same manner that it is the most honorable. But you have come here today for the first time, not as men searching for wisdom, but rather as those standing at the threshold seeking out the handmaids of wisdom, which are the humanities and sciences. I share here the inheritance of Socrates and the complaint which he made against those men who were the first to draw this most dangerous distinction within human society between the two terms "the useful" and "the honorable." That which nature has joined to be one and the same, they have pulled apart by their false opinions.[11] Because this error

---

and the remarkable thing was that in doing this he was putting his wisdom at the service of all his fellow-citizens; and in old days persons resorted to these men both when they were going for a walk as described and when seated in their chairs of state at home, not only to consult them on points of law but also about marrying off a daughter, buying a farm." See also Francis Bacon *De Dignitate èt Augmentis Scientiarum* VIII.2, in *The Works of Francis Bacon*, in 10 vols. (London, 1819), 7.382. Cicero *On Laws* I.33.

11. See Plato *Alcibiades* I.116c–e; Cicero *On Duties* III.11: "And so, we have heard, Socrates used to pronounce a curse upon those who first drew a conceptual distinction between things naturally inseparable. With this doctrine the Stoics are in agreement in so far as they maintain that if anything is morally right, it is expedient, and if anything is not morally right, it is not expedient." Ibid. III.34:

has put down such deep roots in the minds of men, my lecture to you would seem strange indeed if I proposed to show that the death of a noble man is of more value to him than his very life and that an inheritance given freely for the good of all returns to the donor with great increase. Thus I share only in part[12] that Socratic dictum and I would rather say from my own point of view that it is not applicable in those things which are material, either totally, such as money, goods, real estate, or only in part, such as lashings, wounds, murder. But, on the other hand, in those things which are totally of the spirit and dwell in the intellect in which class are contained the liberal arts and the sciences, I would dare to affirm that there can be none that is honorable from which the useful could be separated or distinguished.[13] And indeed none of them

---

"for he has said, not that the truly expedient could under certain circumstances clash with the morally right . . . , but only that what *seemed* expedient could do so. For he often bears witness to the fact that nothing is really expedient that is not at the same time morally right, and nothing morally right that is not at the same time expedient." Ibid. III.101: "People overturn the fundamental principle established by Nature, when they divorce expediency from moral rectitude." Ibid. III.110. *On Laws* I.33: "Consequently Socrates was right when he cursed, as he often did, the man who first separated utility from Justice; for this separation, he complained, is the source of all mischief."

12. [As in a few other instances one encounters within the orations expressions taken from the terminology of the forum. *Dividere sententiam* is an expression that is part of the judicial language of that time and also is used, though rarely, in contemporary legal parlance. Many are the expressions, legal or not, which contain the word *sententia*. Here is a selection: *stat sententia* (it is certain); *ex sententia evenit* (it happened as I thought); *ex animi tui sententia* (according to you); *de sententia deicere* (to change one's mind); *in hanc sententiam abducere* (to come to the opinion); *suas sententias concipere* (make solemn declarations); *quot capita tot sententiae* (there are as many opinions as heads); *per verbum 'videri' suas sententias concipere* (we should express our mind by saying, "It seems to me. . ."). These expressions indicate a respect for the opinions of others, an honest search for truth, and an intention to fight ambitious men, vain men, and those learned men employing their learning deceitfully. See, e.g., Orations I.2; V.8; VI.3.—*Trans.*]

13. See Cicero *On Duties* I.94, III.35: "Again: if we are born for moral rectitude and if that is either the only thing worth seeking, as Zeno thought, or at least to be esteemed as infinitely outweighing everything else, as Aristotle holds, then it necessarily follows that the morally right is either the sole good or the supreme good. Now, that which is good is certainly expedient; consequently, that which is morally right is also expedient." Seneca *Epistles* 120.2–3: "This is what I mean: Some believe the Good to be that which is useful; they accordingly bestow this title upon riches, horses, wine, and shoes; so cheaply do they view the Good, and to such base uses do they let it descend. They regard as honourable that which agrees with the

can generate the greatest utility unless it is directed and ordained toward the honorable. In fact, the liberal professions, which are the product of the mind and spirit, are not of the same sort as life, properties, buildings, so that those who abuse them do not profit from them and those who profit from them do not abuse them. But such professions as these are of a different and wonderful sort, so that those who hoard them do not have them, but those who give them away enrich themselves. It can wittily and truly[14] be said of them that the miserly are poor while the generous are wealthy. And in truth, who is it—the defender or the defended, the ill person or the physician, the counselor or the client—which of the two gains from his efforts—the one who receives or the one who gives? Therefore, if such is the case, then we can necessarily conclude that the more honorable the goal of the liberal profession which one sets for himself the greater would be the profit. What goal is more honorable than to wish to help the greatest number of men and in so doing to become more like Almighty God, whose very nature is to help all? And whoever would desire to be of the greatest service to the greatest number must provide for himself a capacity for such service. Such a one must acquire as much learning as he is capable of by listening as much as possible, by reading

---

principle of right conduct—such as taking dutiful care of an old father, relieving a friend's poverty, showing bravery on a campaign, and uttering prudent and well-balanced opinions. We, however, do make the Good and the honourable two things, but we make them out of one: only the honourable can be good; also the honourable is necessarily good. I hold it superfluous to add the distinction between these two qualities, inasmuch as I have mentioned it so many times. But I shall say this one thing—that we regard nothing as good which can be put to wrong use by any person."

. 14. [About "acuity, keenness, subtlety, shrewdness in speech, sharpwittedness," Vico wrote in *Autobiography*, p. 188, and in the *Institutiones Oratoriae*, ed. Giuliano Crifò (Naples: Istituto Suor Orsola Benincasa, 1989), pp. 282–307. It is in these lessons that Vico presents his students with his views on the *dictum acutum* (a witty saying) as in his orations he shows how to use it in its three constitutive parts—the *res* (the thing), the *verbum* (the word), and the *ligamen* (their connection). In the records of these lessons, which are preserved in the *Institutiones*, we have the list of the different categories of the "witty or acute saying." The *dictum acutum* considered as a genus to different species, may be *argutum, ingeniosum, paradoxicum, ridiculum, sublime,* and *symbolicum*. Among Vico scholars, Michael Mooney in *Vico in the Tradition of Rhetoric* (Princeton: Princeton University Press, 1985) has examined these concepts under the terms *acuity* and *wit.*—*Trans.*]

as much as possible, by analyzing as much as possible, by meditating as much as possible, and by writing as much as possible. And in this way the honorable character, which we have shown to be the principal end of our studies, will be followed naturally by the lesser goals which we have neither proposed nor desired, such as being a source of pride to the sovereign, the pride of the nation, and, in one word, indispensable to the state. Indeed, have you ever seen a learned man who has brought such honor to the kingdom of his prince who has not also been called into the service of that same prince? Have you ever seen a man of letters who has brought honor to the name of his people and who has not also been called to foreign nations with great honors and large sums of money? Have you ever seen a citizen who is reputed to be essential to the state and has not been rewarded with great honors by the state? In truth, O listeners, this is the most close-linked chain of events— from the conviction of desiring to help human society is born duty, from repeated duty is created the reputation of virtue, from that reputation of virtue the praise of the good follows, from the praise of the good men by necessity the power of leadership emerges, then honors, riches, and followers.

[9] How much more honorable and sure is this way than that counsel to dedicate oneself to a goal of corrupt political life which flows from a pristine source but in the stream of wrong consequences becomes muddied and polluted? Such politicians indeed maintain that there is nothing less appropriate to one in politics than to be wholly dedicated to a single goal. But how can this be when the man truly dedicated to public life must be concerned about all things for all people? But then they continue—those who scatter themselves miss many opportunities which arise by chance in the course of events and which might be more useful for affairs that may come up in the future than for those presently at hand. Therefore, they suggest that a man in politics in doing each single thing should conduct himself so that his objectives are directed in such a way that if his first single goal cannot be achieved in full, then a second may be reached, or even a third. If none of these goals can be achieved, then indeed they direct their efforts toward some other goals because, as in nature, so in conducting life, noth-

ing should be without purpose. In this way, therefore, they dispense and distribute the goals so that at the highest level they place titles of honor, below that favor of others, third friendship and renown, and finally the last level should consist of the good opinion of others and dignity for oneself. In this way, they will be thrilled to have been most graciously rewarded when they have received those titles of honor. If that is not possible, they judge that they should at least strive for recommendation and protection which at some time in the future may be useful. If nothing fruitful presents itself, nor even the expectation of an advantage, then they secure for themselves friendship and renown. If nothing firm or likely can be hoped for with which their ambition can be nourished, at least they feel satisfied that their esteem and dignity have been increased. If humor may be permitted in this serious matter, this seems to me to be the ladder which Dante Alighieri describes in his journey to the lower realm by way of which he appears to descend even below the most central point of earth, when in truth he was ascending.[15] Indeed, the highest goal of these politicians is in truth the lowest, and their lowest is actually the highest. Now, I ask you, of these two goals, honor and dignity, which is the more certain and noble? For those who propose as the highest goal of their civic life the acquiring of honor, if by chance they are denied that honor, they abandon all hope and remove themselves from public life. They return to their own interests and live their lives privately. And those who have earned honors but are of a small spirit, like those who become ill from a strong wine, become intoxicated by a small honor and will strive neither by conviction nor industry for something greater. On the contrary, if one has applied all of his efforts to honesty and dignity, if he should not be rewarded, because he is of a noble spirit he will nevertheless continue working for the well-being of the state and eventually will be rewarded with a higher honor which has built up over time. Thus when he has been so honored he will set his sight on an even greater office, stimulated by a strong motivation to achieve it. Since he has acquired this honor he will not think of

15. Dante Alighieri *Divine Comedy: Hell* 34.76–81.

it as a reward from his sovereign for his life of activity but as a pledge to the sovereign of what he intends to accomplish in the performance of his duty. For men of this caliber there is nothing that will befall them for which they are not even more qualified. May I end with one sentence: small roads lead to private homes but royal ways lead to palaces of princes.

[10] And now I would wish that your parents might be present and could hear directly from me how narrow and useless the goal of liberal studies is when it is aimed only to achieve titles of honor. There may even be parents who would propose to their children that the fruits of these studies be some sort of base material gain. And they peddle in public as if in a marketplace the diligent but incomplete studies of their children. In truth, these parents are the reason why the children may not advance any further but continue all their lives in a single position of meager profit. But I have no worries about you who are of noble character and of such promising hopes befitting your age which youth, naturally free of restraints, nourishes. But having said this, what we should rather fear about you is that you might pursue the humane letters with empty goals, leading you to acquire learning for a vainglory. Give up, I pray, this attitude of spirit if any of you is thus inclined. I am not making these remarks to deter you from these studies, but rather I most diligently exhort you, admonish you, incite and stimulate you, since the sciences of government necessary for the operation of the state have reached such an extent of perfection that anyone who would profess them authoritatively must also master these same letters, which one may call the humane letters, totally and deeply. Their handmaidens, indeed, are theology, jurisprudence, medicine, the study of languages, of history, and of eloquence. It is the counsel of the wise that those studies which bear no immediate rewards should be pursued, even though you will be of no help in public life, always pensive at home, never content with yourselves. Nevertheless, in time you will be able to harmonize your studies to the advantage of the commonwealth and your own greatest profit. Finally, I shall conclude with this remark, which, if I am not mistaken, is highly political:—that rulers honor those arts and sciences which bring advantages to the

state and impede the worst evils of the state such as "avarice and excess."[16] Therefore, direct your studies to the common good and on one hand avoid greediness and on the other treat as unimportant those things which are superfluous. I am confident without doubt that you will receive the most meritorious honors, the most well-deserved fortune, the most honestly gained power, the most faithful followers, unswerving gratitude, unflattering praise, and true glory which no force or deceit will alter.

16. Sallust *The War with Catiline* 5.8, 12.2: "As soon as riches came to be held in honour, when glory, dominion, and power followed in their train, virtue began to lose its lustre, poverty to be considered a disgrace, blamelessness to be termed malevolence. Therefore, as the result of riches, luxury and greed, united with insolence, took possession of our young manhood. They pillaged, squandered; set little value on their own, coveted the goods of others; they disregarded modesty, chastity, everything human and divine; in short, they were utterly thoughtless and reckless." Livy *From the Founding of the City,* Preface 11, XXXIV.4.1–2; see also Tacitus *Agricola* 15.4.

On the Liberal Arts
and Political Power

ᘒᘒᘒ

Summary of Oration V

In the fifth oration, delivered in the year 1705, it is proposed "That commonwealths have been most renowned for military glory and most powerful politically when letters have most flourished in them." And the argument is vigorously proved by good reasons and then confirmed by this continuous series of examples. In Assyria there arose the Chaldeans, the first learned men in the world, and there the first monarchy was established. When Greece shone with wisdom more than in all preceding times, the monarchy of Persia was overthrown by Alexander. Rome established her world empire on the ruins of Carthage, whom she destroyed under Scipio, whose knowledge of philosophy, eloquence, and poetry appears in the inimitable comedies of Terence, which Scipio wrote in collaboration with his friend Laelius. (Considering them unworthy to appear under his own great name, he had them published under that of Terence, who doubtless put them into something of his own.) And of course the Roman monarchy was established under Augustus, in whose time all the wisdom of Greece shone forth at Rome in the splendor of the Roman language. The most luminous kingdom of Italy threw out its beams under Theodoric, who enjoyed the counsel of men like Cassiodorus. With Charlemagne the Roman Empire rose again in Germany, because letters, long since dead in the royal courts of the West, began to arise in his in the persons of Alcuin and others. Homer fashioned an Alexander who burned to follow the example of Achilles in valor, and Alexander's example in turn inspired Julius Caesar to great deeds; so that these two great commanders (and none dared say which was the greater) are pupils of a Homeric hero. Two cardinals, both great philosophers and theologians and one of them a great sacred orator as well—Jiménez and Richelieu—drew up the plans for the monarchies of Spain and France respectively. The Turk has founded a great empire on barbarism, but with the counsel of one Sergius, a learned and impious Christian monk who gave the stupid Mohammed the law on which to found it. And when the Greeks, first in Asia and then everywhere, had declined into barbarism, the Arabs cultivated metaphysics, mathematics, astronomy, and medicine, and with this scholarly knowledge, although not with that of the most cultured humanity, they roused to a high glory of conquests the wild and barbarous Al Mansurs, and helped the Turk establish an empire in which all study of letters was abolished. But this vast empire, had it not been for the perfidious Christians, first Greek and later Latin, who supplied it from time to time with the arts and stratagems of warfare, would have fallen to ruin of its own accord. [*Autobiography*, pp. 142–44]

On the Liberal Arts
and Political Power

(Given on October 18, 1705. Argument: "Nations have
been most celebrated in glory for battles and have
obtained the greatest political power when they have
excelled in letters.")

[1]   Much has been discussed by the learned doctors concerning whether the dignity of the literary or of the military arts is the
greater. It is still disputed. Men of letters have brought forth many
arguments both serious and numerous to bolster their literary arts.
Nevertheless, there remain not a few arguments in favor of the
military arts which the men of letters can only with difficulty
refute.[1] Within the military, in fact, it is courage, the most pres-

---

1. The dispute about the preeminence of the liberal over the military arts was
started during the Quattrocento by Bernardo da Siena (1380–1444) in *Commento
ai Trionfi del Petrarca del 'prestantissimo filosofo chiamato Bernardo da Siena. . .
Venexia per Theodorum de Reynsburch et Reynaldum de Novimagio, compagni;
. . . 1478*. Bernardo, in his comments to the work of Petrarch, maintained the
excellence of the military art over the literary because the latter is a benefit to
individuals only, while the former is intended for the good of the commonwealth.
The opposite thesis was offered by Lorenzo Valla (1406–57), *In Sex Libros Elegantiarum Praefatio* (Preface to the Six Books on the Elegance of the Latin Language).
During the Cinquecento the dispute continued, but in a quiet and less effective
manner. Finally, in Muretus (Marc-Antoine Muret, 1526–85), *De Laudibus Lit-
terarum* (In Praise of Letters: Oratio III), the controversy became negligible. He
cited the examples of Caesar and Xenophon and the fact that the inhabitants of
Mytilene used to veto the teaching of letters to the children of the conquered
nations. This thesis constitutes an antecedent to Vico's position in this oration. The

tigious virtue, which transforms men into heroes while the life of the literary man is sheltered and idle.[2] With arms, not letters, empires are founded and increased. Nations powerful in war cause fear in other nations, while those dedicated to the literary arts are open and vulnerable to injuries from others. This is why the prince and the state almost always justly reward the man who distinguishes himself in war with the greatest and most excellent honors. Someone, previously unknown, after one well-done heroic act in battle, receives honors so rapidly that it seems as though he flew to them, while members of an influential household of ancient nobility hardly arrive at such honors even after a long time. And

---

thesis presented and developed here by Vico takes its premises from Muretus and especially from Bacon, *De Dignitate et Augmentis Scientiarum* I, in The Works of Francis Bacon, in 10 vols. (London, 1819) 7:53–107. Bacon's *De Dignitate et Augmentis Scientiarum* was first completed in 1623, but its argument had already been treated in a much shorter form in English in 1605: *The Two Books of Francis Bacon, of The Proficience and Advancement of Learning, Divine and Human. To the King* (J. M'Creery, Black-Horse Court, Fleet Street, London, 1808, pp. 20–21). Here Bacon says: "for experience doth warrant, that both in persons and in times, there hath been a meeting and concurrence in learning and arms, flourishing and excelling in the same men, and the same ages. For, as for men, there cannot be a better, nor the like instance, as for that pair, Alexander the Great and Julius Caesar the dictator; whereof the one was Aristotle's scholar in philosophy, and the other was Cicero's rival in eloquence: or if any man had rather call for scholars that were great generals, than generals that were great scholars, let him take Epaminondas the Theban, or Xenophon the Athenian; whereof the one was the first that abated the power of Sparta, and the other was the first that made way to the overthrow of the monarchy of Persia. And this concurrence is yet more visible in times than in persons, by how much an age is a greater object than a man. For both in Aegypt, Assyria, Persia, Graecia, and Rome, the same times that are most renowned for arms, are likewise most admired for learning; so that the greatest authors and philosophers, and the greatest captains and governors, have lived in the same ages. Neither can it otherwise be: for as, in man, the ripeness of strength of the body and mind cometh much about an age, save that the strength of the body cometh somewhat the more early; so in states, arms and learning, whereof the one correspondeth to the body, the other to the soul of man, have a concurrence or near sequence in times."

2. Bacon *De Dignitate et Augmentis Scientiarum* I, *Works*, 7:64; *The Proficience and Advancement of Learning*, pp. 26–27: "And for the conceit, that learning should dispose men to leisure and privateness, and make men slothful; it were a strange thing if that, which accustometh the mind to a perpetual motion and agitation, should induce slothfulness; whereas contrariwise it may be truly affirmed, that no kind of men love business for itself, but those that are learned; for other persons love it for profit, as an hireling, that loves the work for the wages; or for honour, as because it beareth them up in the eyes of men, and refresheth their

though patrons who support the literary arts reply that if fortitude is a heroic virtue, then certainly prudence is nearly divine because it knows the changing conditions of fortune and transforms chance into the purposeful. They also maintain that it is better to preserve an empire with wisdom than to conquer one with valor. It is better to give reverence to sovereigns than to fear them. They remind us that frequently men of letters have earned the greatest honors and have attained the supreme powers in the state. Nevertheless, their arguments are either frivolous, or unconvincing, or indecisive, so that it cannot yet be determined which of the two arts is superior. Thus, O noble youths, who are led to the highest public responsibilities by the common natural temperament of our nation, and not by necessity or for personal gains but by honesty and for glory, in order to bring to you in support of your studies an argument more solid, more clear and persuasive, I will propose the following: nations have been most celebrated in glory for battles and have obtained the greatest political power when they have excelled in letters.

[2]   Why do I see in your faces that you are surprised and perplexed, O listeners, because I have proposed for your consideration that not only are letters not corrupted by arms, but rather that arms are benefited by letters? This issue has not been brought up before, but listen to its truth with your usual patience and in silence. However, before we leave the shore, the thick cloud of

---

reputation, which otherwise would wear; or because it putteth them in mind of their fortune, and giveth them occasion to pleasure and displeasure; or because it exerciseth some faculty wherein they take pride, and so entertaineth them in good humour and pleasing conceits towards themselves; or because it advanceth any other their ends. . . . Only learned men love business, as an action according to nature, as agreable to health of mind, as exercise is to health of body, taking pleasure in the action itself, and not in the purchase: so that *of all men they are the most indefatigable,* if it be towards any business which can hold or detain their mind" [emphasis added]. See also Cicero *Tusc.* II.27: "But do you note the harm which poets do? They represent brave men wailing, they enervate our souls, and besides this they do it with such charm that they are not merely read, but learnt by heart. Thus when the influence of the poets is combined with bad family discipline and a life passed in the shade of effeminate seclusion, the strength of manliness is completely sapped. . . . We, however, taught no doubt by the Greek example, both read and learn by heart from boyhood the words of the poets and regard such instruction and teaching as a free man's heritage."

arguments arising over this same harbor must be scattered by the rays of the sun if we are to be able to sail forth onto the open sea. In fact, nature has unhappily established that we, by the impetuousness of our mind, fall into error and are brought around to that truth which we are born to reach by a direct path only by a tortuous one. This very situation is what we are now experiencing, since the truth which we have proposed is not reckoned as truth. How can it be, someone would ask, that the great glory of war and the most high praise of wisdom in one and the same commonwealth not only accept one another but accompany and help each other when the military art strengthens the vigor of the body while the discipline of the literary arts weakens it; war arouses, but wisdom tames the spirits; soldiers delight in scuffles, while philosophers love tranquillity; those who are adept at war are wasteful of their souls, while those devoted to wisdom lament the shortness of life because of the plentiful abundance of things to be known;[3] and finally, the arms of warfare prepare the demise of humankind while the arts of wisdom preserve human society? Those who raise these objections to us, of course, would suppose that we are saying that whoever chooses for himself the study of letters also necessarily devotes himself to the military. Nevertheless, what would stand in the way of the wise engaging in battle? Would that these examples become the practice! In fact, the wise would know how to fight for the commonwealth with a different attitude than the one who hires out his soul for cheap gain! But in fact, the study of letters wears away strength,[4] and harsh is the work of the military

3. See Hippocrates *Aphorisms* I.1; Cicero *Tusc.* III.69: "Theophrastus Peripatetic philosopher [pupil of Plato and Aristotle], on the other hand, on his deathbed is said to have reproached nature for having bestowed a long life on stags and crows, creatures to whom such a gift made no difference, whereas mankind to whom it made the greatest difference had so short a time of life bestowed on them: could their life have been prolonged, the result would have been that all systems would have been brought to perfection and human life enriched with the acquisition of all learning. He complained therefore that he was passing away when he had a glimpse of the promised land." Seneca *On the Shortness of Life* 1–2; Diogenes Laertes *Epigrams* V.41.

4. Man in his ascent upward transcends both the mechanical and civil arts by developing the liberal intellectual ones. See Marsilio Ficino *Platonic Theology* XIII.3: "Let us consider therefore those arts which not only are not necessary for bodily nourishment but are very offensive to it, such as all the liberal sciences

in carrying their gear while marching in formation and standing at attention in the sweat of all of the hot days of summer, either at their posts or in performing their duties, and in passing the winter, whenever necessary, lying on the damp earth[5] under a cold sky.[6] All of this is indeed true, but are we not forgetting how great and admirable is the strength of the spirit? Lovers who were lazy and inept by the command of their ladies are transformed into the boldest soldiers and even the most excellent leaders. And now, what are we to think that the wise may do for the love of virtue? Certainly those who think that wisdom is idleness have simply failed to understand it. Wisdom indeed is the improvement of man. And man is mind and spirit. While mind is misled by error, the spirit is corrupted by passions. Wisdom heals both ills, ordering the mind by truth and the spirit by virtue. Virtue, like fire, is forever active and employed in every duty of life.[7] The most important duty is rendering service to one's homeland and the performance of good works for the commonwealth. Why then are the wise idle? So that when it becomes necessary they may find themselves thoroughly prepared. For the same reason they are diligent in their lives so that they may spend them wisely. For them there is no value to their life greater than giving it in service to the commonwealth.

[3] It is not my point that those who are wise also be the military, but rather in that commonwealth where wisdom is held in high regard there is equally great esteem for warfare and mili-

---

whose study enervates the body and restricts the comforts of life. The subtle computation of numbers, meticulous description of figures, the most obscure movement of lines, the mysterious consonance of music, long observation of the stars, the study of natural causes, the investigation of enduring things, the eloquence of orators, the madness of poets—in all of these the soul of man despises the ministry of the body as though he one day would be able and now already begins to live without the aid of the body" [Charles Trinkaus, "In Our Image and Likeness." *Humanity and Divinity in Italian Humanist Thought*, 2 vols. (Chicago: University of Chicago Press, 1970), 1:484–85].

5. Tacitus *Annals* I.17.

6. Horace *Odes* I.1.25: "Many delight in the camp, in the sound of the trumpet mingled with the clarion, and in the wars that mothers hate. *Out beneath the cold sky*, forgetful of his tender wife, stays the hunter, whether a deer has been sighted by the trusty hounds, or a Marsian boar has broken the finely twisted nets" [emphasis added].

7. Cicero *On the Nature of the Gods* I.110: "virtue is in its nature active."

tary power. It is not my intent here to praise the wars of the barbarians to which the barbarians themselves bring the violence of their spirit rather than having been made savage by the wars. This is true unless in your estimation there is no difference whether it is Attila or Xenophon who is waging war. Wherever the Hun brings war, horror overtakes, destruction accompanies, desolation follows; the philosopher, while he is resisted, urges, perseveres; when victory is won, kindness, forgiveness, compassion prevail. Wars of the former kind, in which the greedy fight for blood and gold only to obliterate, exterminate, and plunder, bring ruin to mankind; the latter, instead, in which one confronts the other to set conditions right, is necessary for mankind. What, indeed, do the important standards based on that right mean if not to redress peacefully those injuries by the requital of law, and if it is not possible to do so peacefully then it should be our right to inflict revenge by force to avenge the wrong suffered? And should it not also be our right that soldiers bearing arms uphold and defend the divine law of nations and the supreme rule of the inherent rights of peoples, which is the conserving of human society that the philosophers want to be the standard of all our duties?[8]

[4] From these things about which I have thus far spoken, O listeners, you are aware that by their own natures arms and letters not only do not conflict with one another in ways that will lead the one to rout and destroy the other, but actually they agree so that letters may make known the glory of the military and celebrate the dignity of the military order. However, the issue has not yet been resolved. In fact, in the well-stocked quiver of our adversaries are still many arrows of contention which they can hurl against us. First, they would propose the example of Sparta, which its citizens

8. At the time of this oration, Vico had not yet read the *De Iure Belli ac Pacis* (On the Law of War and Peace) of Hugo Grotius (1583–1645). He tells us in his *Autobiography*, p. 154, that he found himself obliged to read Hugo Grotius in 1715. It is, nevertheless, obvious that Vico at the time of Oration V had indirect knowledge of Grotius's positions. Vico categorizes Orations IV and V by the specific title of *De Finibus Politicis* (On the Political Goals). In fact, in Oration IV he exhorts youth to dedicate themselves to the liberal arts and sciences for the common good of all of society, and in Oration V he explains that the most important of all duties is that of serving the country and of being of value to the commonwealth itself. [See Appendix I.]

defended not by walls but with their bodies, and the boundaries of their domain were defined neither by river nor mountain nor plain nor ramparts, but by the spear. In the field of battle it was their opinion that even the thought alone of fleeing would have been dishonorable. Thus they were accustomed to withhold from the gods even the spoils which they took from the enemy since they were taken from vanquished men, because they believed that to win was in the dictates of fortune and to be won in the power of man. But by what humane learning was so much glory in war sustained? So that they would ignore letters completely and so that there would be no use of them, Lycurgus decreed that not even the laws should be written.[9] I confess that this knot is quite intricate, but I judge it not to be like that of Gordius. In fact, consider what training and discipline they employed to reach their glory in war. The mothers of Sparta would place their unclothed newborn children on a shield; then, they would cause them, when they could walk, to endure, again unclothed, the frigid waters of the Eurotas to harden them for their future military life. Later their fathers, so that their sons might become accustomed to pain and suffering,[10] would flog them as they clung to the statue of Hercules, and often they collapsed unconscious under those strokes.[11] Theft was permitted by their laws so that they could develop dexterity in executing military strategies. By law they were also ordered to die on the field of battle rather than to surrender. Have we truly arrived at the point where the strong earns his true praise of valor by such discipline and the decree of law? Do you not see in these same institutions of the Spartans how a state not established on letters is forced to engage in detestable and harsh practices to earn the glory of battle and to train its generals to command, not according to the honorable qualities of men, but rather to their more base natures?[12] Indeed, I am not even going to speak about the long

9. See Plutarch *Lycurgus* 13.1–4.
10. Cicero *Tusc.* II.36: "the habit of toil renders the endurance of pain easier. . . . It follows that pain sometimes intervenes in these toilsome exercises: the victims are driven on, struck, flung aside or fall, and toil of itself brings a certain callousness to pain."
11. See Plutarch *Lycurgus* 18.2, 17.6.
12. See Plutarch *The Ancient Customs of the Spartans* 25.

duration and vast territory of their dominion, which persisted as long as it was a small part of Greece; but a few years after the Athenians had been defeated in the Peloponnesian War, all the glory of the Spartan empire vanished along with Cleomenes.

[5] But now anyone brought down here by my argument would be able to renew his vigor with an attack brought from the Carthaginian people. Indeed, even though unlettered and lacking experience in any of the humane disciplines and though uneducated in the customs of the Spartans, they fought against the people of Rome with such skill and force that for a long time it was uncertain which would inherit the dominion of the whole world.[13] How many consular armies and how many praetorian cohorts did Hannibal himself massacre? How many banners of cohorts and maniples, how many vexilla of generals, how many eagle insignia of legions did he capture? How many golden rings from the dead of the Roman cavalry did he distribute?[14] How dark for the people of Rome is Lake Trasimeno, how calamitous the River Trebbia, how disastrous Cannae! And now let us ward off this attack. The Carthaginian can number the many defeats suffered by the Romans, but he cannot count triumph over Rome as one of them. Why is that? Why? Compare from each side the reasons for the war. Hannibal assaulted Saguntum in violation of both the divine and human rights of peoples; he defeated and destroyed it, thus creating a pretext for waging war. The Romans, compelled by their pledge of allegiance, were forced into war to avenge the destruction of their ally. Compare the moderation of Scipio in Spain with the shameful behavior of Hannibal among the peoples of Campania, the resolute virtue and prudence of the one with the

13. See Lucretius *On the Nature of Things* III.833–37: "Therefore death is nothing to us, it matters not one jot, since the nature of the mind is understood to be mortal: and as in time past we felt no distress, while from all quarters the Carthaginians were coming to the conflict, when the whole world shaken by the terrifying tumult of war shivered and quaked under the high heaven, and men were in doubt under which domination all men were destined to fall by land and sea; so when we shall no longer be, when the parting shall have come about between body and spirit from which we are compacted into one whole, then sure enough nothing at all will be able to happen to us who will then no longer be, or to make us feel, not if earth be commingled with sea and sea with sky."
14. See Livy *From the Founding of the City* XXIII.12.1–2.

treachery of the other. How great the humanity of the one with which he maintained discipline and fidelity in his army and how cruel the other! Compare Carthage with Rome. Rome even under heavy siege would purchase for a just price the produce of the fields on which the enemies were encamped.[15] Carthage, on the contrary, as soon as it saw the enemy approaching its walls, would fall completely apart. Compare all these things and you would discover with certainty that the true glory in battle can be credited to Rome, but to Carthage, only a shadow of that glory.

[6] By what has been said perhaps someone among you has not yet been convinced and has, in our own time, witnessed the Turkish empire, which never encouraged the study of letters and yet is a great empire respected for its power and famous for its glory in arms. But if Sergius had not impiously abused Christian doctrine in laying down the laws of the Turkish state, and if the Arabs, skilled in letters, had not passed on their best military traditions, and if new implements of warfare and new techniques of assault and conquest of cities had not been forthcoming from us, then what?[16] Would I be able to say that today we would have no enemy in all the world greater than this empire?

---

15. Ibid. XXVI.11.5–6: "he learned from a prisoner that about this time the land on which he had his camp chanced to have been sold, with no reduction in price on that account. But it seemed to him so arrogant and such an indignity that a purchaser should have been found at Rome for the ground which he had seized in war and was himself its occupier and owner."

16. [On the topic of these lines see A. Garzya, "Vico, l'empio Sergio e lo stupido Maometto," *Bollettino del Centro di Studi Vichiani* X (1980): 138–43. The *hadith* literature contains several variations of the Sergius legend. The earliest is that of ibn Hisham (d. ca. 833 A.D.). Some accounts refer to him by the Arabic name Bahira (the chosen), but others refer to him by the Christian name Sergius, and still others as Georgius. A Christian version of the eleventh or twelfth century, the Bahira Apocalypse, may have been the source of the Sergius reference used by Vico. See H. Gottheil, "A Christian Bahira Legend," *Zeitschrift für Assyriologie*, vol. 13; *Shorter Encyclopaedia of Islam*, p. 55. See also Sergius and Bahira in Philip Khuri Hitti, *History of the Arabs* (London: Macmillan, 1958), p. 111. Sergius or Bahira, therefore, must have lived during the lifetime of the Prophet Muhammad. Vico used "stupido Maometto" in his *Autobiography* to render in brief the phrase found in Ludovico Marracci's *Alcorani textus universus in Latinum translatus . . .* (Padua, 1698), I.36: "Mahumetus homo idiota et legendi scribendique prorsus ignarus" (Muhammed, an uneducated man and certainly incapable of reading and writing).—*Trans.*]

[7]   And now, as I understand, something similar is happening to me as to those who would open for themselves a way direct as that of the birds and then, by the same effort in removing obstacles, have accomplished a leg of their journey. In fact, when we have scattered those objections which have obstructed our proposed argument we have at the same time proved the central point of it, namely, that the study of the liberal arts contributes exceedingly to the military arts. And now then, if we want to investigate fully the reason for this, if I am not mistaken, it should become evident that wars are a kind of judgment of law. You may be puzzled at this new definition. Listen to the reasons. Man has a dual citizenship, one of which has been given to him by nature, the other by the conditions of his birth.[17] The limits of the former are the heavens, those of the latter are precisely defined. Each of them is based on its own laws, the first by the divine right of nations, the other by the proclamation of the people, the senate, or the sovereign. In each there is fellowship among men, in one by alliances among nations, in the other by common consent. If private parties bind themselves by contract or have violated the law, our rights with them can be protected by specific legal procedures. However, if a people has violated the divine right of nations or has broken a treaty of alliance, then what sort of remedy will shine forth to preserve the law of human society? War and the implements of war. If, therefore, the guardians of civil law profess a true, not false, philosophy; if the legitimate commonwealths are only those which are founded on laws that the wise have created; if Cicero, the greatest of philosophers, considered the simple book of the Twelve Tables above all the libraries of philosophers;[18] then, given that the universal right of the people is superior to the civil right inasmuch as the whole of mankind is valued more than any single

17. Seneca *Epistles* 4.1: "Keep on as you have begun, and make all possible haste, so that you may have longer enjoyment of an improved mind, one that is at peace with itself. Doubtless you will derive enjoyment during the time when you are improving your mind and setting it at peace with itself; but quite different is the pleasure which comes from contemplation when one's mind is so cleansed from every stain that it shines." See also Philo Judaeus *On Husbandry* 196e–197a [and n.38 to Oration II—*Trans.*].
18. Cicero *On the Orator* I.195.

national unit, how much of the knowledge of the military art, which is the science of human rights, do we think is necessary in order to achieve perfect glory?

[8] And truly, O listeners, it becomes necessary that the supreme commander of the army be crowned with the following virtues rather than decorated with an ostentatious helmet and crest—with justice, so that the reasons for war be just; with moderation, so that he would practice forgiveness as well as wrath; with restraint, so that he may extract from the defeated no more than what would threaten; with clemency, so that he would keep the captives alive rather than annihilate them. Among his troops, he is accessible; among the pacified, he is harmless; in the presence of the enemy, he is of unswerving command. These are the virtues of the spirit that wisdom confers on the supreme commander. Consider now those of the mind. Dialectic provides him with cautiousness of judgment so that he may avoid surprise ensnarements. Geometry teaches the design of the camp and the battle order of the troops in a circle, then dispersed, then in square and finally in wedge-shaped formation as conditions require. By arithmetic he can establish the number of the enemy from the location they occupy. Optics allows him to estimate from a distance the height of fortifications and the length and duration of a march. Architecture erects the arches, builds the walls of defense, the ramparts, and excavates the trenches. Mechanics contributes to the inventions of artillery, and moral philosophy aids him in knowing the customs and nature of the people. The lessons of the past will enable him to know what to avoid and what to pursue. Eloquence gives him the means to arouse the reluctant to battle, to encourage those who are dispirited in defeat, to restrain the exuberant in victory. How much utility the natural sciences contribute to the military arts is confirmed by the example of the leader who accounted for the causes of the eclipse of the moon or sun to his frightened troops and thus urged them on to greater feats.[19]

19. See Aeneas Sylvius Piccolomini (1405–64), *Treatise on the Education of Children*, in *Aeneae Sylvii Piccolominei Senensis, . . . , Tractatus de liberorum educatione . . .* in *Opera . . . Basileae, ex officina Henricpetrina, s.a. (saec. XVI)*, p. 990. Quintilian *Rules of Rhetoric* I.10.46–49 mentions the importance of the

Where can those virtues of mind and spirit so numerous and great
be found if not in the people of those commonwealths established
by the wisest according to the best precepts of peace and war, and
which the most learned have conserved by the cultivation of letters
as the best principles of the commonwealth? From this I am of the
opinion that the wisest among the poets have transmitted into the
tradition through their myths that one and the same goddess is
represented in Minerva and Pallas Athena. From this I think that
the Athenians, who were the most perceptive of men, honored
Minerva, whom they considered the goddess of wisdom, as the
founder and protectress of their citadel in order to set forth this
truth imagined and concealed in myth—it is for the same commonwealth to excel in letters in times of peace and in arms in times
of war.

[9]   But if it is necessary that the future commander completes
a cycle of so many and such important sciences, certainly his talent
for war, which is the only talent that can equip him mentally with
the ability of judgment in the midst of horrors and destruction,
would be greatly diminished. This argument is as weak as an
arrow of figwood.[20] Indeed, we should not expect to find them all
in the same supreme leader of the war, but we would look for them
within the council of advisers of the supreme leader, so, if it should
happen that they are not all in his possession, which would be
ideal, they will at least be accessible to him when the need arises.
The truth is this—those people who are uncultivated in letters and
deprived of the valued customs of peace and war are like a herd of
cattle. And if by chance they want to become renowned in the art
of warfare it would be necessary for them to employ a force of
multitudes. And if they should overcome nations more cultured
than they, it would be required, in order to govern securely, that
either they master arts and letters along with the conquered or else
destroy those arts and letters. In fact, the natural talents are

knowledge of astronomy for the formation of the perfect orator. Piccolomini in the
treatise, however, considers that astronomy is especially useful for future kings and
commanders of armies. He dedicates his treatise to Ladislaus V, king of Bohemia
and Hungary, and Vico makes reference to the kings of Hungary in paragraph 10 of
this oration.

20. See Horace *Familiar Talks* I.8.1.

whetted by the study of letters, and those nations so honed are like the pugilist who does not strike down by force but rather, at the right moment, trips up the adversary by his maneuvering.

[10] We are now speaking in praise only of the military arts, not of the floods of disaster and desolation, nor of the founding of great empires, nor of the destruction of cultured states, nor of Alexander, nor Caesar, nor of the barbarous leaders of savage peoples. A people cultured in letters, though they nevertheless be properly ordered solely by the institutions of peace, and though detesting war, as long as they are secured either by natural or manmade protections, are prevented by nothing from setting up a large and prosperous dominion if within the legitimate limits of their rule they are afforded vast expanses of land. Let us give as an example the Chinese before the Scythians burst through their great wall. Indeed, unlettered people, to whom the wise have left behind the most worthwhile institutions of peace and war, while those institutions are alive and the times foster conformity to them, because neither is constant, can amass for themselves extensive dominions through the great power of war either only for a short time or never at all. Now since the unlettered are inexperienced in the letters from which they could have learned new military techniques, but nevertheless they seek to extend their dominion, in case their enemy has progressed in the military arts, they might find themselves confronted by a people of valor and skill which has a somewhat higher knowledge of letters and more experience in warfare even though inferior in arms and power such as the kings of Hungary, who stopped the expansion of the Turkish monarchy. If, on the other hand, they are assaulted by new and unfamiliar techniques of war, without doubt they would be toppled like all empires that have fallen under attack by an enemy using battlefield strategies never before encountered, or new weapons of war, since they did not have the ability that comes from having obtained command of letters enabling them to imitate the enemy, or because they have lacked an alternate skill in the art of effectively outmaneuvering the enemy.

[11] But neither the practice of peace or war, though the best, could achieve without the most dedicated pursuit of letters the

highest glory in war and the establishment of monarchies, since the most crucial aspect of warfare is to know the moment to launch the battle. Concerning such matters, here as in all other instances that depend on wise choices, there can be no established rule. In fact, if there were precise rules and one sought to invoke them, given that rules are finite but circumstances infinite, if you wait for the right moment when the circumstances conform to the rules, that moment of winning will pass you by and you will be crushed by your enemy. Because of this we never read of these monarchies being born out of times of peace, but rather founded through war and battles. Only the philosophers, however, can discern the best of circumstances because only they know things as they are. Indeed, the two most renowned of all commanders of armies are Alexander the Great and Julius Caesar.[21] Alexander became the Great because he modeled himself after greatness, stimulated by his reading of the example of Homer's Achilles.[22] Caesar vied with Alexander for virtue and praise due a commander because of his reading of the deeds of Alexander, which drove him to emulate the example of the greatest of military leaders.[23] Thus we can justly trace the renown of Alexander and Caesar to Homer, which means to say, the literary arts. In fact, we perceive that in the flow of history there is an order such that where the literary arts have flourished so too have the glories of the military arts. When Greece flourished in all manners of sciences and arts, it also excelled in military power. When Rome shone forth in the study of wisdom, it also exhibited brilliance in warfare. The study of letters during the Dark Ages of the Christians found a place among the Arabs, and they became celebrated for the glory of their arms. When the Christians again took up the study of letters, cultivated and nourished them, they became among all peoples of the world the most renowned in the art of warfare. In those nations within which wisdom stood one would therefore expect the world's monarchies to have been founded. Writers of their history

21. See Bacon *De Dignitate et Augmentis Scientiarum* I, *Works*, 7:60. See also note 1 above.
22. See Plutarch *Alexander* 8.2.
23. See Plutarch *Caesar* 11.5–6.

numbered them as four. Determine for yourselves whether their selection is correct. Among the Assyrians it was the Chaldeans who reigned as the wise in that realm, and then soon after Ninus founded the first of the monarchies.[24] Among the Persians the Magi, who were the wise among them, sustained the land, and then Cyrus established the second.[25] Among the Greeks were the greatest and most brilliant of philosophers, and consequently the dominions of the world were focused on them. The study of letters among the Romans was most carefully cultivated and celebrated by all, and there appeared Augustus, "who chose to limit his empire by the ocean and his fame by the stars."[26]

[12] Because the cultivation of the fine arts can contribute so much to the glory and greatness of arms and empire, as I have shown, if you, O youth, are attracted by my words to the study of these arts, direct your attention here. This university of studies is the temple wherein the military disposition may be cultivated. By these studies, indeed, the wisdom necessary to the military is nurtured. And then from you will come forth a noble feeling for arms, from you the best planning of strategies, from you the finest abilities of leadership, and finally from you will come glory in war and greatness of empire.

24. See Cicero *On Divination* I.2: "Now I am aware of no people, however refined and learned or however savage and ignorant which did not think that signs are given of future events and that certain persons can recognize those signs and foretell events before they occur. First of all—to seek authority from the most distant sources—the Assyrians, on account of the vast plains inhabited by them, and because of the open and unobstructed view of the heavens presented to them on every side, took observations of the paths and movements of the stars, and, having made note of them, transmitted to posterity what significance they had for each person. And in that same nation the Chaldeans—a name which they derived not from their art but their race—have, it is thought, by means of long-continued observation of the constellations, perfected a science which enables them to foretell what any man's lot will be and for what fate he was born." See also ibid. 91.
25. See ibid. I.46.90–91.
26. Virgil *Aeneid* I.287.

On the Proper Order of Studies

❧❀❧

Summary of Oration VI

In the sixth oration, delivered in the year 1707, he treats of this
argument, which is partly on the ends of the various studies and
partly on the order of studying them. "The knowledge of the
corrupt nature of man invites us to study the complete cycle of the
liberal arts and sciences, and propounds and expounds the true,
easy and unvarying order in which they are to be acquired." In it
he leads his hearers to meditate on themselves, how man under
pain of sin is divided from man by tongue, mind and heart. By the
tongue, which often fails and often betrays the ideas through
which man would but cannot unite himself to man. By the mind,
through the variety of opinions springing from diversity of sensu-
ous tastes, in which men do not agree. And finally by the heart,
whose corruption prevents even the conciliation of man with man
by uniformity of vice. Whence Vico proves that the pain of our
corruption must be healed by virtue, knowledge and eloquence;
for through these three things only does one man feel the same as
another. This brings Vico to the end of the various studies, and
fixes the point of view from which he considers the order of study.
He shows that as the languages were the most powerful means for
setting up human society, so the studies should begin with them,
since they depend altogether on memory which in childhood is
marvelously strong. The age of childhood, weak in reason, is regu-
lated only by examples, which to be effective must be grasped with

vividness of imagination, for which childhood is marvelous. Hence children should be occupied with the reading of history, both fabulous and true. The age of childhood is reasonable but it has no material on which to reason; let children then be prepared for the art of good reasoning through a study of the quantitative sciences, which call for memory and imagination and at the same time check the tendency to corpulence of the imaginative faculty, which when swollen is the mother of all our errors and woes. In early youth the senses prevail and draw the pure mind in their train; let youths then apply themselves to physics, which leads to the contemplation of the corporeal universe and has need of mathematics for the science of the cosmic system. Thus by the vast and corpulent physical ideas and by the delicate ideas of lines and numbers let them be prepared to grasp the abstract metaphysical infinite by the science of being and the one. And when they have come to know their mind in this science let them be prepared to contemplate their spirit and in consequence of eternal truths to perceive that it is corrupt, so that they may be disposed to amend it naturally by morality at an age when they have had some experience of the evil guidance of the passions, which are most violent in childhood. And when they have learned that by its nature pagan morality is insufficient to tame and subdue philauty or self-love, and when by experience in metaphysics they understand that the infinite is more certain than the finite, mind than body, God than man (who cannot tell how he himself moves, feels or knows), then with humbled intellect let them make ready to receive revealed theology, from which let them descend to Christian ethics, and thus purged let them finally pass to Christian jurisprudence. [*Autobiography*, pp. 144–45]

On the Proper Order of Studies

꒰Ꙭ꒱

ORATION VI

(Given on October 18, 1707. Argument: "Knowledge of
the corrupt nature of man invites the study of the entire
universe of liberal arts and sciences, and sets forth the
correct method by which to learn them.")

[1]   The situation of adolescents who have to be educated in
the liberal arts and sciences most certainly seems difficult to me,
given that their parents, who neither have knowledge of such
things nor even inquire of those who do have such knowledge,
without exploring the inherent constitution of their children and
without discerning their native talents, push the youth to study
one or another of the arts and sciences, most often contrary to
their inclination, on the grounds of their own desires or to satisfy
family needs.[1] Or if naturally inclined to these studies they are

1. Cicero *On Duties* I.110: "Everybody, however, must resolutely hold fast to
his own peculiar gifts, in so far as they are peculiar only and not vicious, in order
that propriety, which is the object of our inquiry, may the more easily be secured.
For we must so act as not to oppose the universal laws of human nature, but, while
safeguarding those, to follow the bent of our own particular nature; and even if
other careers should be better and nobler, we may still regulate our own pursuits by
the standard of our own nature. For it is of no avail to fight against one's nature or
to aim at what is impossible of attainment. From this fact the nature of that
propriety defined above comes into still clearer light, inasmuch as nothing is proper
that 'goes against the grain,' as the saying is—that is, if it is in direct opposition to
one's natural genius." See also Horace *Art of Poetry* 385.

often pushed into them without adequate preparation in related studies.[2]

"Here there are tears, here there is misery,"[3] when, deprived of those studies which are necessary for the discipline to which they are applying themselves, they advance not at all or only a little and then with great difficulty. Attributing it to a fault in their own character, when it is rather a mistake of the parents, they lose all hope of acquiring that discipline. Even if they succeed in becoming more learned whether or not they share the goals of their parents, the parents force them into the study of jurisprudence to bring honor to the family. But because they are of a timid and shy nature they care little for clients, or high offices, or public responsibilities. Parents, desiring great financial gain, push their sons into the medical arts, but because of their higher aspirations they instead behold with admiration those most respected gentlemen who occupy and serve in the various offices of the commonwealth. Hence it happens that as long as the respect due to their fathers binds them, they continue to pursue those studies unwillingly and with disdain and do not cultivate them either seriously or with enthusiasm. At the first opportunity to be free from the bond of filial devotion, having abandoned entirely and put behind them the study of the liberal arts, they pass their lives in idleness and some even in immoral conduct. But if there is someone, as becomes a courageous man, who will persist on the road he has entered, and under the unwise pressure of his parents having learned nothing methodically and all against his natural disposition, now at a difficult age when he may have family as well as public responsibilities, he must learn the same things by himself. In this process so many and so formidable difficulties stand in his way that most men would be left with nothing more than a bitter longing for a sounder education.

[2] Meanwhile, I have often myself thought about this inconvenience or, rather, misfortune. I have accused nature by which it has been arranged that man must choose his vocation in life at an

2. Plautus *The Little Carthaginian* 312.
3. Terence *The Lady of Andros* 126.

age when he knows nothing about anything and has no basis for choosing. While I was investigating the reasons for this, I recalled to myself that the beginning and source of all evils is the sin of Adam and the original corruption. However, when I thought about this more deeply, I saw myself to be unjust.[4] Indeed, if we ourselves contemplate our own corrupted human nature we will discover that it not only points out to us those studies which we must cultivate but will also clearly disclose the order and path by which we shall approach them. These are the two most important topics that we shall now consider.

[3] And if I say that each of you must search within himself in order to consider carefully his human nature, he will in truth see himself to be nothing but mind, spirit, and capacity for language. Indeed, when he analyzes his body and its functions he will judge it to be either that of a brute or in common with the brutish. From this he will note that man is thoroughly corrupted, first by the inadequacy of language, then by a mind cluttered with opinions, and finally a spirit polluted by vice.[5] He will observe that these are the divine punishments by which the Supreme Will[6] punished the sin of the first parent so that humankind who descended from him will become separated, scattered, and dispersed. For having introduced so many families of languages as a punishment to the impious Nimrod[7] and having spread them throughout all the world, he caused nations to be separated from nations. With the flow and flux of time which changes every language, he also willed that

4. See ibid. 378.

5. Lucretius *On the Nature of Things* V.1031: "But the various sounds of the tongue nature drove them to utter, and convenience pressed out of them names for things, not far otherwise than very speechlessness is seen to drive children to the use of gesture, when it makes them point with the finger at things that are before them."

6. [We have translated *summum Numen* as "Supreme Will" though it could be translated otherwise. Vico wanted to express the immediacy and facility with which God can act from within nature itself, even human nature, because of the *originis vicium*. In his book on metaphysics of 1710, *On the Most Ancient Wisdom of the Italians*, Vico explains *numen* together with *fatum* (fate), *casus* (chance), and *fortuna* (fortune) and says of them that they *consentiunt*, that is, agree or act together for the same goal.—*Trans.*]

7. [Nimrod was the great-grandson of Noah (*Gen.* 10:8) and the first king of Babel in the land of Shinar.—*Trans.*]

within those nations the language of the fathers become unknown to their descendants. Moreover, having introduced opinions in which there is only a semblance of truth, passion, according to the inclination of each person, will lay hold of it as a truth. And, therefore, to each his own opinion and as it is commonly said—as many heads, so many opinions.[8] Finally, so great is the baseness of vice that those who are vicious make every effort not to look upon their own. They detest those of others, and the same vices which are in us are those we reproach in others. Thus the miserly wants nothing to do with the miserly and the unjust man complains of being wronged by another unjust man.[9] God does not will that any society be founded upon vice, not even one of the vicious among themselves.

[4] Even more to the point, because of the fault of the original parent, as I have said before, the Supreme Will inflicted the same punishments in an unfortunate manner on each and every man as he did in scattering mankind. Hence, since man's language in almost all situations is inadequate, it does not come to the aid of the mind and even fails it when the mind seeks its help in expressing itself. Because speech is awkward and uncultivated, it corrupts the meaning of the mind with words that are without merit. With words that are obscure, it betrays it, or with words that are ambiguous what we say is misunderstood or stumbles over itself by the very words which are spoken. To these deficiencies of language are added those of the mind. Dullness constantly grips the mind. False images of things toy with it and very often deceive it. Rash judgments cause the mind to form hasty conclusions.[10] Faulty reasoning lays hold of it, and finally this confusion of things baffles and bewilders it. But, by Hercules, how much more grave are the shortcomings of the soul which are churned up by every storm and flux of the passions more turbulent than those of the straits! Thus it burns with desire and trembles in fear! It becomes dissipated in pleasures and is given to weakness in pain! It desires all things but never finds delight in any choice! What it once disapproved it now

8. See Terence *Phormio* 454.
9. See Terence *The Lady of Andros* 639.
10. See ibid. 214; Sallust *The War with Jugurtha* 63.6.

approves, what it now disapproves it once approved![11] It is constantly unhappy with itself, always running away from itself and yet seeking itself! Moreover, self-love, as its own tormentor, makes use of these wicked plagues and tortures. Because basic human nature has been changed by original sin, assemblies of men may appear to be societies, but the truth is that isolation of spirits is greatest where many bodies come together. Even more is it like the crowded inmates of a prison where the spirits that I have mentioned above endure punishments, each in the cell to which it is assigned.[12]

[5] I have enumerated as the punishments for corrupted human nature the inadequacy of language, the opinions of the mind, and the passions of the soul. Therefore, the remedies are eloquence, knowledge, and virtue. These three are like the three points around which all the orb of the arts and sciences encircles. All wisdom is contained in these three most excellent things—to know with certainty, to act rightly, and to speak with dignity.[13] Such a man as that would never be ashamed of his errors, never repentant for having acted viciously, never regretful of having spoken without propriety and decorum. He is without doubt a true man whom the Terentian character describes neatly, "I am a man, and nothing human is foreign to me."[14] Chremes—not for hope of

11. See Horace *Epistles* I.1.98.

12. See Plato *Phaedo* 62b, 67c–d, Plato (Pseud.) *Axiochus* 365e; Cicero *Scipio's Dream* 14; *Tusc.* I.75: "is severance of the soul from the body anything else than learning how to die? Let us, therefore, believe me, make this preparation and dissociation of ourselves from our bodies, that is, let us habituate ourselves to die. This will, both for the time of our sojourn on earth, resemble heavenly life, and when we shall be released from our chains here, the progress of our soul will be less retarded. For they who have always been caught in the shackles of the body, even when they are set free, advance more slowly, like men who have been many years bound with chains. And when we have come yonder, then and not before shall we live; for this life is indeed death, and I could sorrow over it if so I would." Lactantius Firmianus *Divine Institutes* VII.8.

13. Gerhard Johannes Voss (1577–1649), *Gerardi Ioannis Vossii De Ratione Studiorum nec non Introductio in Chronologiam*, in *G. I. Vossi et aliorum Dissertationes de studiis bene instituendis. Traiecti ad Rhenum, typis Theod. Achersdyk et Gisb. Zylii, anno 1658* (p. 22) wrote: "Three are the virtues of the one who has finally reached a cultured level—he should be capable of understanding, be wise and speak correctly" (our translation).

14. Terence *The Self-Tormentor* 77: "*Mene*—Chremes, have you so much time to spare from your own affairs that you can attend to another man's with which

gain, not out of necessity, not out of indebtedness, but simply in a neighborly spirit—asks Menedemus, who plays the part of the fool, tormenting and punishing himself, the reasons why he does this: "Don't cry! Help me to understand what bothers you! Don't conceal it! Don't be afraid!"¹⁵ And he promises him the following: "Trust me, I say! I will help by conforting and advising you and will support you!"¹⁶

[6] Three are the very duties of wisdom—with eloquence to tame the impetuousness of the fools, with prudence to lead them out of error, with virtue toward them to earn their goodwill, and in these ways, each according to his ability, to foster with zeal the society of men. Those who do these things are indeed men much above the rest of mankind, and, if I may say, only a little less than the gods. A glory neither counterfeit nor transitory but solid and true follows such men. Certainly a fame based on merits so great which others cannot reach will be known far and wide. For no other reason, the very wise poets created their poetic fables of Orpheus with his lyre taming the wild animals and Amphion with his song able to move the stones, which arranged themselves of their own accord by his music, thus erecting the walls of Thebes.¹⁷ For their feats, the lyre of the one and the dolphin of the other have

you have no concern? *Chr.*—I am a man, I hold that what affects another man affects me. You may take it that I am offering advice or asking a question, which you like, so that if you are right I may do as you, if you are wrong I may scare you out of this. *Mene*—I have got to do this; *you* may do what you find necessary for your own case. *Chr.*—Has any man got to torment himself? *Mene*—I have."

15. Ibid. 84–85: "If you have some cause of distress, I am sorry; but what is it? What's the trouble? Please tell me what grievous crime you have committed against yourself."

16. Ibid. 86: "Don't weep, tell me your trouble whatever it is: don't be reserved or afraid. Trust me, I say; you'll find I can help you either by consolation or by advice, possibly by direct assistance."

17. See Horace *Art of Poetry* 391–96; Ovid *Treatise on Roman Calendar* II.79–118: "The Dolphin, which of late thou dist see fretted with stars, will on the next night escape thy gaze. (He was raised to heaven) either because he was a lucky go-between in love's intrigues, or because he carried the Lesbian lyre and the lyre's master. What sea, what land knows not Arion? By his song he used to stay the running waters. Often at his voice the wolf in pursuit of the lamb stood still, often the lamb halted in fleeing from the ravening wolf; often hounds and hares have couched in the same covert, and the hind upon the rock has stood beside the lioness: at peace the chattering crow has sat with Pallas' bird, and the dove has been neighbour to the hawk." Herodotus, *History* I.23–24.

been hurled into the heavens and are seen among the stars. Those rocks, those oaken planks, those wild animals are the fools among men. Orpheus and Amphion are the wise who have brought together by means of their eloquence the knowledge of things divine and human[18] and have led isolated man into union, that is, from love of self to the fostering of human community, from sluggishness to purposeful activity, from unrestrained license to compliance with law and by conferring equal rights[19] united those unbridled in their strength with the weak.[20]

[7] This is always the truest, greatest, and most excellent goal of these studies. Many choose not to pursue them but are rather moved by the false, the base, and the abject, and because they are moved by the false, the base, and the abject it follows necessarily that they apply themselves to these studies falsely, basely, and abjectly. Here I could easily account for such people, but for reasons of honor, I will not mention them. However, on this subject I should give you a brief comment. He who in these studies is not seeking wisdom, that is, who does not cultivate these studies in order to improve his character and inform his mind with truth, his spirit with virtue, and his speech with eloquence so that he becomes constant with himself as a man and, as much as possible, able to help human society, is often other than what he professes to be. He is frequently speechless about much that is necessary to the very art which he professes. He often loathes, and neglects, and

18. See Cicero *The Divisions of Oratory* 79: "For eloquence is nothing else but wisdom delivering copious utterance; and this, while derived from the same class as the virtue above that operates in debate, is more abundant and wider and more closely adapted to the emotions and to the feelings of the common herd. But the guardian of all the virtues, which shuns disgrace and attains praise in the greatest degree, is modesty." See also *On the Orator* II.187; Pacuvius *Hermiona* 177: "And you may think I'm craven dull or tongue-tied."

19. See Cicero *On Invention* I.2; *On the Orator* I.33.35; III.76; *On the Nature of the Gods* II.148.

20. Livy *From the Founding of the City* I.7.5; VII.5.6. On the allegorical interpretation of the myth of Orpheus and Amphion see Horace *Art of Poetry* 391–407; Dante *Convivium* II.1; Petrarch *Letters to Family Members* I.9.7; Petrarch *Rime* 28.68–72. Vico himself, in his commentary on Horace's *Ars Poetica*, Nicolini, *Vico. Opere*, 7:75–76, after having repeated the comment of Augustine in the *City of God* XVIII.14, reminds his readers that the first stage of human reason is of a poetic nature and refers to the *New Science* pars. 81, 523, 661, and 734.

corrupts the very art which he professes. But in truth, he who in wisdom applies himself to correct his corrupted nature always acts with all the techniques of his art in which he has been instructed, he always acts with zeal and seriousness, he always acts in accord with the proper purpose of his own art. And in the community where those who profess their arts for the sake of the truth only, and only for the well-being of humanity, how flourishing are its citizens, how fortunate the commonwealth, I shall, to be brief, leave for you yourselves to think about!

[8] Having established that the same consideration of corrupted humanity has admonished us to embrace the whole sphere of human arts and sciences, let us now see in what order it dictates to us that we should learn them (which will be the other part of my argument). And so that you can more easily understand it, I should at the beginning explain what constitutes wisdom and the means toward its end.

[9] Wisdom, as is frequently said, consists in the knowledge of things divine and prudent judgment in human affairs and speech that is true and proper.[21] But even before true and effective principles concerning language, it is necessary that we first have speech that is grammatically correct. What then follows is knowledge of the divine, which here I understand and speak of as, first, those things for whom nature is God and are called natural things, and, second, those things for whom God is the nature and are properly called divine things. We consider among natural things those which have been already fully accepted by man, namely geometric figures and numbers from which mathematics constructs its own demonstrations, and also causes which are most frequently debated among the learned doctors and are investigated by physics. Under physics I include anatomy, which is the study of the fabric of the human body, and that part of medicine which inquires into the causes of illness and which is nothing else than the physics of

21. See Cicero *On Duties* I.153: "the foremost of all virtues is wisdom . . . ; for by prudence, . . . , we understand something else, namely, the practical knowledge of things to be sought for and of things to be avoided. Again, that wisdom which I have given the foremost place is the knowledge of things human and divine, which is concerned also with the bonds of union between gods and men and the relations of man to man."

the diseased human body. That which provides the treatments of illnesses is indeed properly called the art of medicine and is an effective corollary of the integration of physics and anatomy, such as mechanics is the practical application of the integration of physics and mathematics. Divine things, however, are the human mind and God. Metaphysics studies both in order to contribute to science, while theology studies them in order to contribute to religion. Therefore, with these doctrines the knowledge of all things both natural and divine is completed. Wise judgment in human affairs requires that each perform his duties as man and as citizen. Moral doctrine renders man virtuous, civil doctrine makes of him a wise citizen, and both, when adjusted to our own religion, form that theology which is called moral theology. These three doctrines come together and unite in jurisprudence. Jurisprudence is indeed almost exclusively composed of moral doctrine because it is neither a science nor an art but is the knowledge of right, and its intent is justice; of civil doctrine, because it is concerned with advantages to the public; and of moral theology, because we are interpreting the right within a Christian commonwealth. Hence about things divine and human, we either debate among the learned or converse among the common man, and with the former it is necessary that we discourse in truth, and with the latter it is necessary that we use a speech that is appealing. Truth is the purpose and goal of logic in speech, while rhetoric teaches an appealing way of speaking free from meter, and an appealing speech in verse is the purpose and goal of the art of poetry.[22]

[10] Now it is necessary that you know that almost all of the arts and sciences which I have mentioned have their own written histories, and as methodologies provide the general principles of things, the several histories authenticate them with specific examples. The most able writers in each language make up the history of languages. From these writers the best examples to establish

22. Notice Vico's similarity to Voss's *De Ratione Studiorum* (On the Method of Studies), pp. 5–6: "Philosophy essentially is made of prudence and wisdom. Wisdom is reflection on nature and like medicine, as I stated before, relies on nature; prudence deals with the moral and civil disciplines. From the latter jurisprudence is derived. Eloquence teaches one to speak properly in order to persuade and does it in prose with an oration, as in oratory, or in a poem, as in poetry."

how this or that people spoke have been transmitted, and the most famous orators and poets are the exemplars in the art of oratory and poetry. Concerning physical phenomena, histories have been written and continue to be written every day. And what about the observation and the recording of illnesses and the devising of certain pharmaceuticals which the common man refers to as some specific medication? Are they not commentaries on physics and the art of medicine? And does not mechanics write of the histories of new inventions of war, navigation, and architecture? By no means would you be wrong in calling histories of dogmatic and moral theology those which transmit the dogmas of faith revealed by the supreme God and the regulations of customs which are prescribed from one time to another. Certainly theologians counted the sacred books for the most part as historical. And is not the ecclesiastical tradition an uninterrupted and continuous succession of ecclesiastical doctrine and discipline? Commentaries, annals, records of the lives of famous men and of public affairs—are they not parts of the moral and civil doctrines so that they can properly be called by a most precise term, history? Truly, the histories of jurisprudence encompass those laws which have been promulgated within the commonwealth from time to time, and the interpretations given to them by the jurisconsults and the examples of legal decisions which have been rendered. Pure mathematics, by contrast, has no history because specific examples are unnecessary, and neither does logic because it uses examples from other disciplines. When examples are lacking, it constructs them.[23] Even less does metaphysics have a history because it studies the human mind and God as the purest and simplest of natures and nothing else.

[11] At this point I derive from the Greeks that division by which all disciplines separate the esoteric from the exoteric, but I understand them differently.[24] The esoteric disciplines are those which must be heard from teachers in order to be more easily

23. This statement, too, is taken from ibid., p. 14.

24. See Gellius *Attic Nights* XX.5.1–4: "The philosopher Aristotle, the teacher of king Alexander, is said to have had two forms of the lectures and instructions which he delivered to his pupils. One of these was the kind called 'ecsoterika' or 'exoteric,' the other 'akroatika,' or 'acroatic.' Those were called 'exoteric' which

acquired, and I understand them as the methods and principles of study of the arts and sciences. The exoteric, which truly each of us is capable of learning by himself, are those disciplines which are derived from the recorded histories of the arts and sciences.

[12] Therefore, all the store of the human arts and sciences having been made accessible so that we may learn them to attain wisdom, we must follow our own corrupted nature as a guide. There is no doubt that childhood is an age when reason is much weaker while memory is so much stronger. In fact, children of three years of age already have all the words and all the expressions necessary for everyday life which a voluminous dictionary would hardly be able to contain. There is no discipline which needs reason so much less and memory so much more than language. In fact, language is based on the common agreement and usage of the people, "among whom there is the choice of the rules and norms of speech."[25]

Therefore, there is no other age better than childhood for learning languages. And here one of you will ask, Which languages are the best to devote ourselves to learning? That same knowledge of our corrupted nature will answer this question. In fact, among the particular punishments which I have identified, I list the roughness, the diversity, and the obscurity of languages which have torn apart human society. These defects have to be remedied by the teaching of languages, which as far as possible should be polished, unambiguous, and communal so that by this human society may again be embraced.[26] Of these languages, there are two. One is Greek and the other Latin. Both are unambiguous, but Greek is

---

gave training in rhetorical exercises, logical subtlety, and acquaintance with politics; those were called 'acroatic' in which a more profound and recondite philosophy was discussed, which related to the contemplation of nature or dialectic discussions. To the practice of the 'acroatic' training which I have mentioned he devoted the morning hours in the Lyceum, and he did not ordinarily admit any pupil to it until he had tested his ability, his elementary knowledge, and his zeal and devotion to study. The exoteric lectures and exercises in speaking he held at the same place in the evening and opened them generally to young men without distinction. This he called . . . 'the evening walk,' the other which I have mentioned above . . . 'the morning walk'; for on both occasions he walked as he spoke. He also divided his books on all these subjects into two divisions, calling one set 'exoteric,' the other 'acroatic.' "

25. Horace *Art of Poetry* 72.
26. *Institutiones Iustinianae* III.27.6.

the more learned while in these days Latin is the more widespread. Therefore, youths must apply themselves to these two, and beyond this, so that they better understand the meaning of the sacred books which are the principal instruments of Christian theology, it would be helpful to them also to master the sacred language.

[13] Having left childhood behind, the human mind, which is reason, begins to emerge from the mire of matter. Moreover, we say that opinions are punishments inflicted on the mind because of original sin. Therefore, corrupted nature demands that opinions from these early years must be overcome. And yet phantasy in youth is most vigorous. Proof of this would be that when we are young we make up opinions of distant cities and regions which are later difficult to dispel and replace with other images. So deeply are they engraved that it would hardly be possible to erase them completely and build others in their place. Nothing is more adverse to reason than phantasy. (We experience this in women, in whom phantasy prevails and reason is used less. Because of this they are plagued more than men with violent and confused emotions.) This being the case with phantasy, it is necessary that we imitate the medical doctors who use dangerous poisons in proper dosages for illness and in this manner heal. <u>Phantasy must shrink so that reason will be strengthened.</u> Adolescents, therefore, must apply themselves to mathematics, which is a discipline still very much aided by the ability to construct images.[27] Often, for example, it is necessary to picture in the mind a very long series of forms or numbers in order to construct a proof and arrive at the truth of the conclusion. By doing this the human mind cleanses and purifies itself when it considers points and lines which have neither thickness nor body. And in this way, youths become accustomed to derive from those things which have been agreed upon among men a truth from a given truth so that in physics, which is the most debated of the disciplines, they can apply a similar method. Advancing in maturity and in the use of mathematics, the human mind becomes progressively more free from the body and acts in a rational manner, and from things which are perceived by the senses it is able to gather together those things which escape all

27. See Plato *Republic* VII.521c–d, 522b–c, 526a–c.

sensations even though they are still substances.[28] And so we move from mathematics to physics, which considers those substances that are not perceived by the senses and their figure and motion, which are not perceptible but are the principles and causes of natural phenomena. And so the human mind is purified by means of mathematics and physics from grossness and denseness of thinking so that it gradually reaches the contemplation of incorporeal realities and with an uncontaminated and pure intellect comprehends itself and through itself Almighty God. The human mind will be led from the known facts of mathematics to the doubtful in physics to metaphysics, which seeks out those realities which are true, certain, and thoroughly known. Having then reached metaphysics and having acquired possession of the rules concerning the false, the probable, and the true, at this point the very art of oratory is appropriate for the purpose of interpretation. Then having known Almighty God, whom nature discloses, may you seek to reach that level of the knowledge of Him which our religion teaches and may you turn your mind to Christian theology.

[14] Wise judgment concerning human affairs follows the acquisition of the perfect knowledge of things divine. In the ordering of these disciplines we must imitate those who plot the course of ships, and as they observe the heavens, the pole star, and other stars so as to hold to a steady course through the oceans and steer safely to their harbors, so we contemplate divine things, the human mind, and the supreme God, and we use the knowledge of them as the Ursa Minor so that we may steer the course of human life cautiously and securely through the shoals of opinion, the shallows of doubt, and the hidden rocks of error. Since fools do not have the skill of knowing the true, they are ignorant of the true limits that set apart good from evil, which is the knowledge of the source of all human practical wisdom.[29] There are many evil things that appear to be good. In contrast, there are many good things that give the appearance of evil, and those who are imprudent in these things follow the pleasures of the body and abhor

28. Lucretius *On the Nature of Things* I.269–70.
29. Cicero *On the Greatest Good* I.12.

work, poverty, and the death of an honest man. Consequently, they afflict themselves with their own vices and corrupt the society of men. For this reason, corrupted human nature longs to know because it longs to be happy. Those who have not ordered their literary studies for the gaining of wisdom as the source of human happiness may cast off the punishments inflicted on language or mind but still have not freed the spirit from those punishments. For this same reason, there are indeed most learned men who, however, are driven around in circles by ambition, anxiously living for the fleeting glory of their erudition and burning with jealousy for those who are more learned than they. And so it happens that they propose for themselves as goals those studies which are the means to achieving wisdom. The true function of the disciplines which I have previously proposed is to accustom the mind to true things, so that as soon as it is so accustomed, it may enjoy them. And thus, because man desires the true, he can do the good easily, and when he is in the habit of doing it, he chooses over all else the true goals of all good things in the conduct of his life, that is, the virtues and the good arts of the spirit, and through them he cultivates the divinity of the mind, and by means of the mind, reaches God. Therefore, having been imbued with the knowledge of divine things, may you learn prudence in human affairs, first, the moral, which forms man, then the civil, which forms the citizen. In this way, having expertise in them, you will easily apply yourselves to moral theology so that in the future you will be able to guide princes as their advisers in ordering and administering public affairs with the wisest of counsel. Consequently, you will act in a most expedient manner in learning jurisprudence, which almost all would derive from moral and civil doctrines and from the dogmas and customs of the Christians. Finally, you have been instructed in these studies of wisdom so that each of you may earn merit far and wide from human society and be of help, not only to yourselves or to a few, but to as many as possible, and to this end you should join with these studies those of eloquence.[30] Indeed, let

30. [Vico is here introducing what is essentially the main point of the seventh inaugural oration of 1708, *On the Study Methods of Our Time*, pp. 37, 49. In that oration, in brief, he shows how the fusion of philosophy and eloquence happened

none of you fear, when all of these studies for the cultivation of wisdom have been pursued, that he will grow old in learning them from the learned teachers. He will become old, most certainly he will become old, if he cultivates them without the proper instruction, if he cultivates them not in accord with their purpose, and if he cultivates them in an inappropriate sequence. Fabius Quintilian eloquently refers to this as wasting time by taking shortcuts.[31] More acutely and no less true, if I am not mistaken, you might have said, They stand still because they rush ahead. And how is it that there are so many obstacles to no one more than to the one who hurries? Those who follow a confused order of studies move as though in a labyrinth and fail to progress. The shortest way of all is the direct way and the advantage of having an order is to complete the most in the shortest period of time. Because these studies, which are joined by nature and which we have arranged in the order that I have explained, have been split up and confused by the foibles of men, they appear to be many, but in reality they are not many but are one and the same perceived in many different lights. All the principles of the arts and the doctrines of the sciences which we have judged to be esoteric and to be learned from the teachers, if nothing foreign from other disciplines is added to them, are all very short. (What need is there to introduce anything if all else has been taught in its proper sequence?) We have judged that the histories of the sciences and the arts are exoteric and so it is possible that you can learn them by yourselves.

[15] Moreover, O youth of great hope, the counsel which I

in the classic periods of Greece and Rome and how that fusion produced jurisprudence. Jurisprudence, indeed, became wisdom—the knowledge of things divine and human. For Vico's explanations of philosophy, eloquence, rhetoric, jurisprudence, and wisdom see also "The Academies and the Relation between Philosophy and Eloquence," trans. Donald Phillip Verene, in *On the Study Methods of Our Time* (1990) and *Vico. Institutiones Oratoriae*, ed. Giuliano Crifò, chaps. [1–9].— Trans.]

31. Quintilian *Rules of Rhetoric* I.4.22: "Boys should begin by learning to decline nouns and conjugate verbs: otherwise they will never be able to understand the next subject of study. This admonition would be superfluous but for the fact that most teachers, misled by a desire to show rapid progress, begin with what should really come at the end: their passion for displaying their pupils' talents in connexion with the more imposing aspects of their work serves but to delay progress and their short-cut to knowledge merely lengthens the journey."

give you is to follow the most excellent goal and method of studies. In fact, if you consider this by the light of honesty, you will find it the most excellent, if by the light of utility, the best, and if for ease of learning, the most expedient. This is the advice which I am not ashamed to have given, because, though I be not wise, I have followed those who are. If they always act because they have the ability to act, I, for my part, have said those things because of the prodding of my corrupted nature. I have done that in this oration because it is as much as I may seriously and diligently do for you according to the proper object of my profession and according to my part as a man in serving human society.

Appendix I

❧

Goals of the Various Studies
Suitable to Human Nature

Oration I

Let us constantly cultivate the divine force of our mind.

Oration II

Let us fashion our spirit by virtue and wisdom.

Oration III

(which may be considered an appendage to the previous
two orations)

Let us shun feigned and idle learning.

POLITICAL GOALS

Oration IV

Let everyone be educated for the common good of
the citizenry.

Oration V

Let us increase the glory of arms and the grandeur of
political dominion with learning.

[Vico wrote this schematic presentation of the arguments of the orations between
April or May 1709 and February 1710. It was intended as the table of contents of
the book he was hoping to publish. The completed manuscript included all seven
orations given between 1699 and 1708. See Benedetto Croce, *Bibliografia
Vichiana*, rev. and enlg. by Fausto Nicolini, 2 vols. (Naples: Ricciardi, 1947–48),
1:11.]

Christian Goal

Oration VI

Let us cleanse corrupt human nature and, as much
as possible, thus help human society.

On the Method of Studies

(in the same oration)
Let us embrace the method of studies that corrupt
nature dictates.

A Dissertation[1]

more comprehensive has been given to the printers
about the manner in which the disadvantages of our
method of studies could be surmounted when
compared with the one of our ancients,
so that ours would result in a method more direct
and preferable to theirs.

1. This publication in the early part of 1709 is *On The Study Methods of Our Time*, which is the seventh oration, given in 1708.

Appendix II

꧁꧂

History of the Latin Manuscripts

(abridged translation of
Gian Galeazzo Visconti's introduction)

1. The Manuscript Tradition of the "Inaugural
   Orations"

Vico, as professor of rhetoric at the Royal University of Naples,
between 1699 and 1707, on the feast of Saint Luke, October 18,
gave an oration in Latin at the convocation that opened the academic year. A total of six orations, commonly known as the *Inaugural Orations*, have been preserved in the codices described below.[1]

1. [It was Vico's task as professor of rhetoric to offer the formal greetings of the
university to incoming students as well as to authorities of government and church
and important visitors. In compliance with a custom at the University of Naples,
the professor of rhetoric was also required to deliver the address solemnizing the
opening of each new academic year. The speeches given at these convocations came
to be known as "inaugural" orations. The Italian expression "le orazioni inaugurali" was first introduced in 1914 by Fausto Nicolini in the title of Volume 1 of
Opere di G. B. Vico, ed. Fausto Nicolini (8 vols. in 11) (Bari: Laterza, 1911–41).
Benedetto Croce stated that there were six speeches given by Vico which are
customarily called "inaugural orations." He lists their titles (*argumenta*) and the
years when they were delivered on the Feast of St. Luke, October 18, as 1699,
1700, 1701, 1704, 1705, and 1707. See Benedetto Croce, *Bibliografia Vichiana*,
rev. and enlg. by Fausto Nicolini, 2 vols. (Naples: Ricciardi, 1947–48), 1:9, 80.
The oration known as *De Nostri Temporis Studiorum Ratione*, given on November
1, 1708, which we have, is in the form of a treatise that Vico himself, shortly after
the address, rewrote and published five months later, in April or May of 1709.

Appendix

(a) The first MS., named D (Naples, National Library Vittorio Emanuele III, XIII B 55), contains the six *Orazioni Inaugurali* (inaugural orations) and the *De Nostri Temporis Studiorum Ratione* (On the Study Methods of Our Time) with Vico's own marginal and interlinear corrections. It is a paper codex of the seventeenth century with sixty-nine sheets originally unnumbered, which after 1914 were progressively numbered by the curators of the National Library of Naples. Sheet numbered 1 on the recto contains Vico's original dedication to the Capuchin friar Francesco Antonio Ceraso da Palazzuolo and on the verso a brief summary of the six orations and the *De Nostri Temporis Studiorum Ratione*. Sheets numbered 2 to 59 on the recto are by the hand of Vico's brother, the notary Giuseppe, and contain the six orations and the *De nostri temporis ratione studiorum*. The *emendationes* (corrections), in Vico's hand, of Orations I–V are found in the smaller sized sheets numbered 60 on the recto to 66 on the verso. Sheet 67 has been added by the binder and is blank; sheets 68–69 are also extraneous to this codex.

(b) In the second MS., named C (Naples, National Library Vittorio Emanuele III, XIII B 36), is found the dedication that Vico wrote for Duke Marcello Filomarino Della Torre, to whom he sent Oration II on December 1, 1708. Sheets 3–4 constitute this dedication while sheets 5–18 contain Oration II. The remainder of the MS. contains letters of Cardinal Jacopo Sadoleto. It is also a paper codex, smaller than the previous one, made of thirty-two originally unnumbered sheets, later numbered in pencil up to sheet 19.

Croce does not seem to consider it an "inaugural" oration in its present form; neither does Gian Galeazzo Visconti. On the contrary, Elio Gianturco, *On the Study Methods of Our Time*, calls it "the seventh in the series of his (Vico's) 'inaugurals.'" Lucia M. Palmer, *On the Most Ancient Wisdom of the Italians*, shares Gianturco's opinion: "Vico delivered seven inaugural addresses. Of the seven only the last one, *De Nostri Temporis Studiorum Ratione*, was published during his life-time, the other six remained in manuscript form until the middle of the nineteenth century." Palmer does not mention the *De Mente Heroica*, which Gianturco instead identifies as "Vico's last inaugural, his eighth," and which was addressed to the audience on October 20, 1732. Croce referred to this oration as being "the last, it seems, of those recited by Vico." The criterion of distinction between the first six and the last two has been based on the fact that the latter two, not long after they were delivered in public, were reworked and significantly modified, finally being published for the wider audience of readers.—*Trans.*]

It has been determined to be by the hand of the erudite Neapolitan Gian Vincenzo Meola (1744–1814) and is based on an antique autograph copy of Vico.

Both MSS. D and C represent a text of the first six orations that had been carefully revised by Vico and therefore is different from the original that he read at the convocations. This original text unfortunately has been lost. It should be identified as "a." The *emendationes* themselves are direct and convincing proof of the changes wrought by Vico, which are not simple corrections of wording but true modifications of concepts. The *emendationes* constitute a pamphlet of seven sheets attached to MS. D (60r–66v) and are, as we said previously, by the hand of Vico. It is possible to affirm that these corrections were drafted after October 18, 1706, the date of his reading the fifth oration, and completed before the end of 1707. It has been concluded through a philological analysis that these *emendationes* do not refer to the transcription of the orations in MS. D, though they have been attached to it, but to a prior version that may very well be the original version revised by Vico. That is the lost document "a."

Vico persistently retouched his orations using the *emendationes* and version "a," drafting what we can assume to be identifiable as MS. "b," which has also been lost. From "b" Vico copied the second oration and sent it on December 1, 1708, to Duke Marcello Filomarino Della Torre, hoping that he would publish it. Vico, therefore, must have been working on "b" between October 18, 1707, and December 1, 1708. In "b" we have the common source of all the "inaugural orations" that, together with the *De Nostri Temporis Studiorum Ratione*, were being copied between April or May of 1709 and the first months of 1710 by Vico's brother Giuseppe. It was Giambattista's intention to publish them as a small volume that treated the goals and method of all studies, *De finibus et ratione studiorum* (On the Goals and Method of Studies). Vico, indeed, dealt with the goals and purposes of all branches of learning in his orations and explained the study methods to be used in the oration of November 1, 1708. At this time, however, only the *De nostri temporis ratione studiorum* was given to the printers by the publisher Felice Mosca in March or April of

1709. Thereafter, Vico seemed to have lost all hope of publishing his orations all together as a general treatise. In fact, within MS. D, after Oration III, there are no longer visible signs of editing or indications that would lead us to think of Vico's continuing interest in publication.

Vico's most dynamic thought evolved gradually and consistently. Finally, he

> came to perceive that there was not yet in the world of letters a system so devised as to bring the best philosophy . . . into harmony with a philology exhibiting scientific necessity in both its branches, that is in the two histories, that of languages and that of things. . . . By this insight Vico's mind arrived at a clear conception of what it had been vaguely seeking in the first *Inaugural Orations* and had sketched clumsily in the dissertation *On the Study Methods of Our Time*, and a little more distinctly in the *Metaphysics*.[2]

With the continuing cooperation of the publisher Felice Mosca, in 1725 Vico published a book entitled *Principles of a New Science of the Nature of Nations, from Which Are Derived New Principles of the Natural Law of Peoples* (known as the "First New Science"), and "in this work he finally discovers in its full extent that principle which in his previous works he had as yet understood only in a confused and indistinct way."[3]

The inaugural orations, which were the works of Vico's youth in which he had searched for that principle, had by now become unimportant and he "was therefore glad that he had not published these orations, for he thought the republic of letters, stooped under so great a pile of books, should not be burdened with more, but should only be offered books of important discoveries and useful inventions."[4]

These orations, however, had their own value. In the same way in which he could recognize the origins of the humane and civi-

2. *Autobiography,* pp. 155–56.
3. Ibid., p. 166.
4. Ibid., p. 146.

lized nations within their nascent period, so Vico could now realize that from the time of the first oration he "was agitating in his mind a theme both new and grand, to unite in one principle all knowledge human and divine."⁵

The orations constituted the first germ, the first point of departure, of the long process of growth and development of his thought. The history of this thought was contained in the *Autobiography*. In it, Vico included extensive summaries of the orations, copying them directly from MS. D.

In this way, the orations, though in a summarized form, were to be published as part of his autobiography, and, having no longer need of MS. D, Vico sent it again as a present to the Capuchin friar Palazzuolo on June 23, 1725.

2. The Printed Editions of the "Inaugural Orations"

The digest made by Vico for the *Autobiography*, published at Venice in 1728, may very well be considered the first printed edition of the *Inaugural Orations*. Vico's old wish had been fulfilled as he personally desired to include some significant new parts in Latin, which are the *argumenta* and the *recitatio* of Oration II.⁶

The oration that first had a true and proper publication was Oration II. It was edited by the Marquis of Villarosa and published in the fourth volume of his *Vici Opuscula* (Vico's Short Works) in 1823. Villarosa could use only MS. C and, therefore, published a piecemeal oration. He has the merit of having justly corrected some parts of the text and of being the first to publish an inaugural oration. Villarosa's publication still retains too many

5. Ibid.
6. Ibid., pp. 139–45.
[The *argumenta* are the titles that announce and put down in concise form the theme of each oration. They are found in the *emendationes* which are a part of MS. D and from which Vico transcribed them into his summary of the orations in the *Autobiography*, pp. 140–45. See also Croce, *Bibliografia Vichiana*, p. 9.

Recitatio, in general, refers to an oral reading of a judicial document and Vico, by using this word, introduced within the text of the second oration what he considered the laws of nature to be followed by man in order to achieve wisdom. See Oration II, par. 2.—*Trans.*]

textual deficiencies and, therefore, was not considered in Visconti's reconstruction of the Latin text.

Oration II was again published twice in 1835 by Francesco Predari in the only volume of his *G. B. Vico, Opere* (Vico's Works) and afterward by Giuseppe Ferrari in Volume 6 of his collected works of Vico (Milan, 1835–37). Both publications, however, only reproduced Villarosa's text with the addition of a few corrections and variants. Ferrari's efforts, all things considered, resulted in the better of the two editions.

Ferrari's edition of Oration II was again reprinted in Naples in 1840 by Enrico Amante in cooperation with the printer Giuseppe Iovene in the volume entitled *Opusculi Vari di Giambattista Vico* (Various Short Works). Amante unfortunately tried to combine Ferrari's and Villarosa's editions into a variant that was worse than the original publication by Ferrari.

The edition of Oration II by Francesco Saverio Pomodoro for the printers Domenico and Antonio Morano (Naples, 1858) was more faithful to Ferrari's version and better than the one made by Amante. He, too, tried to parallel the Ferrari and the Villarosa texts, combining what he thought correct. It was included in the volume titled *Autobiografia, Della Antichissima Sapienza degl'Italiani ed Orazioni Accademiche di Giambattista Vico* (Autobiography, On the Most Ancient Wisdom of the Italians and Academic Orations). The book was in Italian with the Latin text at the foot of the page. In short, of the six orations, only Oration II, thanks to MS. C, went in one variant or another to the printers and saw different editions and publications between 1823 and 1858.

In the year 1861 MS. D was found in the library of the Capuchin Friars at the Monastery of St. Efrem. Antonio Galasso, librarian at the National Library of Naples, took the necessary care for the publication of Vico's five unedited orations that were believed to have been lost (I, III, IV, V, VI), the *emendationes*, and the beginning part of Oration II that was lacking in MS. C. Galasso printed his work as *Orationes Quinque Ineditae* (Five Unpublished Orations) in Naples in 1869, paying the Fratelli Testa Editori out of his own pocket. Under pressure from the Fratelli Morano Editori, also of Naples, Galasso prepared a second printing of the book, but this time with an Italian title, *Cinque Orazioni Latine Inedite* (Five Unpublished Latin Orations). Together with a long introduction, it was published as Volume 7 of Morano's edition of Vico's complete works also in 1869. The year 1914 saw another Latin edition of Vico's orations within the series Scrittori d'Italia, *G. B. Vico, Opere* 1 (Bari: Gius. Laterza & Figli). This critical edition, prepared with scholarly accuracy by Giovanni Gentile and Fausto Nicolini, is superior to all previous editions.

3. Studies and Translations of the "Inaugural Orations"[7]

Galasso's edition of the five orations, which had never previously been published, did not receive due attention. Carlo Cantoni reviewed it very briefly, and Benedetto Croce in his book on Vico's philosophy dedicated only one page to it. Robert Flint and Giovanni Gentile, on the contrary, considered it with keen attention and penetrating intelligence.[8]

The *Inaugural Orations*, after the 1914 publication of the Latin

7. [The present work constitutes the first translation for the English-speaking community of Visconti's reconstructed Latin text and subdivision into paragraphs. Visconti's translations have also helped. In fact, Gustavo Costa in his review of Visconti's book said that "Visconti's translations, coming after those of S. Mazzilli, E. De Falco, and A. Fratoianni, are elegant and precise" (*New Vico Studies* 2 (1984): 171). The oration recited in 1708 titled *De Nostri Temporis Studiorum Ratione* has been translated by Elio Gianturco as *On the Study Methods of Our Time* (New York: Bobbs-Merrill/Library of Liberal Arts, 1965). It has been reprinted with the addition of "The Academies and the Relation between Philosophy and Eloquence," trans. Donald Phillip Verene (Ithaca: Cornell University Press, 1990). The oration *De Mente Heroica*, given on October 20, 1732, has been translated by Elizabeth Sewell and Anthony C. Sirignano as "On the Heroic Mind" in *Social Research* 43 (Winter 1976): 886–903, and again in *Vico and Contemporary Thought*, ed. Giorgio Tagliacozzo, Michael Mooney, and Donald Phillip Verene (Atlantic Highlands, N.J., and London: Humanities Press and Macmillan, 1979), pt. 2, pp. 228–45.—*Trans.*]

8. [Carlo Cantoni, *G. B. Vico* (Turin: Civelli, 1867); Benedetto Croce, *The Philosophy of Giambattista Vico*, trans. R. G. Collingwood (New York: Russell and Russell, 1964); Giovanni Gentile, *Studi Vichiani* (Florence: Sansoni, 1968); Robert Flint, *Vico* (Edinburgh: Blackwood, 1884). Palmer correctly remarks: "Benedetto Croce pays no attention to these early speeches and begins his study of Vico with the *De Antiquissima* . . . whereas . . . Giovanni Gentile considers the orations the first stage of Vico's philosophy" (*On the Most Ancient Wisdom of the Italians*, p. 9n).—*Trans.*]

critical edition by Nicolini and Gentile, attracted large and enthusiastic interest from many scholars. The important studies of Benvenuto Donati, Enzo Paci, Antonio Corsano, Guido De Ruggiero, Nicola Badaloni, A. Bernardini and G. Righi, A. M. Jacobelli Isoldi, Eugenio Garin, Paolo Rossi, Biagio De Giovanni, and Giuseppe Giarrizzo are here mentioned in chronological order. These scholars have dealt effectively with the problem of Vico's early intellectual development in the years during which he delivered the earlier orations.[9]

Philological studies of the Latin text of the orations have been very limited. The only scholars paying some attention to this have been, in chronological order, Fausto Nicolini, Marcello Gigante, and Salvatore Monti. Fausto Nicolini has given the best philological reconstruction of Vico's text, influencing the studies of Giovanni Gentile. Marcello Gigante has demonstrated that the rules for a critical edition of Vico's Latin text must be equivalent to those used by the humanists of the Quattrocento and Cinquecento. He has also recommended systematic research to identify the sources and thus indicate the historical development of Vico's Latin writings. Salvatore Monti offered a philological study of Vico's orations, and his work constituted the definitive source for the preparation of the critical Latin edition made by Gian Galeazzo Visconti.

The translations of the *Inaugural Orations* into other languages have not been as numerous as those of other writings of Vico. In fact, only Stefano Mazzilli, Enrico De Falco, and Aldo Fratoianni have ventured to make an Italian translation. Stefano Mazzilli has translated not only the orations but also the *De Mente Heroica* (Florence, 1941), facing the difficulties presented by the text of Fausto Nicolini's Latin edition. Enrico De Falco has dealt specifically with the pedagogical aspects of the orations, translating Orations I, II, V, and VI for a text to be used by students enrolled in programs for teachers' training (Naples, 1954). Aldo Fratoianni's translation is the most valuable because it is clear, readable, and

9. [For a detailed analysis of the works of these scholars, see the complete references that Gian Galeazzo Visconti gives, *Le Orazioni Inaugurali, I-VI*, pp. 30–32.—*Trans.*]

more closely adheres to the Latin text. It has been published by Sansoni Editore with Nicolini's Latin edition side by side (Florence, 1971).[10]

4. Vico's Orthography, the Scribe of MS. D and the Greek Terms

The Vichian Latin orthography in the *Inaugural Orations* presents its own variations and difficulties of interpretation. For example, Vico constantly writes "author" and "authoritas" instead of "auctor" and "auctoritas" etymologically deriving the former from the Greek term "autos." He explains his preference by saying that "author" means the man who can express his own uniqueness, that is, all that is divine and human within him. He also accepts the spelling "caussa" with the double "s" because that was the Roman usage during the most splendid period of the empire and is documented by the inscriptions on stone monuments.

MS. D prefers the spelling "coelum" instead of "caelum," "coelestis" instead of "caelestis." This spelling of the word is also preferred by the *Etymologicon* of J. Voss (Amsterdam, 1662), which Vico certainly consulted. Vico also made a distinction between "cum" and "quum" following the examples of Quintilian and Aeneas Sylvius Piccolomini. He used "cum" as a preposition before a noun in the ablative case and "quum" as a temporal conjunction introducing a temporal clause with the verb in the indicative mode. Both MSS. C and D observe this distinction. The consistency is broken by MS. D in two instances, in Orations IV and V, but whenever these passages are quoted they appear in a corrected form, showing that in D they amounted to simple orthographic errors. MS. D presents another Vichian preference of "qui" with circumflex accent to signify "quomodo."

The scribe of MS. D is accused by Nicolini of having little knowledge of Latin and even less of Greek. In fact, this scribe left spaces between words whenever a Greek term was supposed to be copied. Nicolini later on identified Vico's brother Giuseppe as the

10. Ibid., pp. 33–36.

scribe. Further research, however, has proved that even though Giuseppe Vico, a notary, was deficient in classical Greek, the errors incorrectly attributed to him in copying were mostly due to his brother's correct and authentic "lectiones" (readings, interpretations).[11]

11. Ibid., pp. 41–42.

List of Sources Cited

Sources refer to divisions and lines as numbered in Loeb Classical Library editions where such editions exist; otherwise to other standard editions of the original texts. Orations are referred to by i, ii, iii, iv, v, vi and footnote number.

Aristotle
  Poetics: 1457b, 20–22: i. 20n
Arrian, Flavius (of Nicomedia, modern Izmet)
  Epicteti Dissertationes (Discourses of Epictetus):
    II.19.12–17: iii. 8n
    III.15.3: iii. 32n
Augustine
  Confessiones (Confessions): X.8.14: i. 24n
  De Civitate Dei (City of God):
    III.21: ii. 27n
    VIII.5: i. 17n
    VIII.11: iii. 45n
    XVIII.14: vi. 20n
    XVIII.42: iii. 45n
    XXII.20: i. 12n
Bacon, Francis
  De Dignitate et Augmentis Scientiarum (Of the Proficience and Advancement of Learning):
    I, pp. 53–107: v. 1n
    I, p. 60: v. 21n

I.58, 61: i. 6n
I.59: i. 9n
I.61: ii. 40n
I.94: i. 32n
II.18–19: ii. 9n
II.19: i. 17n
II.21: ii. 53n
De Natura Deorum (On the Nature of the Gods):
I.72: iv. 8n
I.79: ii. 49n
I.110: v. 7n
II.45: i. 7n
II.62: i. 17n
II.148: vi. 19n
II.153: ii. 44n
II.154: ii. 38n
III.74: iii. 41n
De Officiis (On Duties):
I.13: i. 31n
I.18, 94: i. 32n, iii. 30n
I.51: iii. 31n
I.57: iv. 6n
I.81: ii. 51n
I.94: iii. 30n, iv. 13n
I.110: vi. 1n
I.153: ii. 41n, vi. 21n
II.39–40: iii. 10n
II.40: iii. 11n
II.43: iii. 53n
III.11, 34: iv. 11n
III.35: iv. 13n
III.39: iii. 16n
III.55: iii. 31n
III.60, 61: iii. 41n
III.61, 70: iii. 20n
III.101, 110: iv. 11n
De Oratore (On the Orator):
I.33, 35: vi. 19n
I.195: v. 18n
II.187: vi. 18n
II.194: i. 36n

V.70: i. 6n
V.108: ii. 40n
Verrem (Actio in) (Against Verres): IV.53: iv. 1n
Dante, Alighieri
Convivium: II.1: vi. 20n
Inferno (Divine Comedy: Hell): 34.76–81: iv. 15n
Demosthenes (Pseudo-)
Orations: 25.16: i. 25n
Diogenes Laertius
Lives of Eminent Philosophers (Epigrams):
V.41: v. 3n
X.13: iv. 8n
Ficino, Marsilio
Epistolarum Libri (Books of Epistles): I.1: i. 6n, 12n, 28n
Prohemium in Platonicam Theologiam (Preface to the Platonic Theology): I.15–17: i. 6n
Theologia Platonica de Immortalitate Animorum (Platonic Theology on the Immortality of Souls):
XII.3: iii. 5n
XIII.3: i. 19n, v. 4n
XV.5: i. 13n
Gellius, Aulus
Noctes Atticae (The Attic Nights):
I.2.6: iii. 8n
X.26.1: iii. 15n
XX.5.1–4: vi. 24n
Herodotus
History: I.23–24: vi. 17n
Hippocrates
Aphorisma (Aphorisms): I.1: v. 3n
Horace, Quintus Flaccus
Ars Poetica: Ad Pisones (Art of Poetry: Epistle to Piso):
72: vi. 25n
243: i. 2n
296–97: i. 36n
385: vi. 1n
391–96: vi. 17n
391–407: vi. 20
404: iii. 31n
413: iii. 32n
Carmina (Odes):

Longinus (Pseudo-)
De Sublime (On the Sublime): 12.4: iii. 13n
Lucretius, T. Carus
De Rerum Natura (On The Nature of Things):
  I.73: i. 18n
  I.73.1102: ii. 36n
  I.75–77: ii. 50n
  I.80–81: ii. 5n
  I.142: iv. 3n
  I.269–70: vi. 28n
  II.57–58: ii. 22n
  II.1045, 1144: ii. 36n
  III.16: ii. 36n
  III.89–90: ii. 22n
  III.833–37: v. 13n
  III.1053–70: ii. 3n
  IV.1131–34: ii. 19n
  IV.1153–70: ii. 49n
  V.89–90: ii. 50n
  V.119, 454, 1213: ii. 36n
  V.1031: vi. 5n
  VI.37–38: ii. 22n
  VI.64–66: ii. 50n
Marcianus Capella
Digesta: De Legibus et Senatus consultis et longa consuetudine (Digest: On the Laws and Decrees of the Senate and on the Established Practice): I.3.2: i. 25n
Ovid, P. Naso
Fasti (Treatise on Roman Calendar):
  II.79–118: vi. 17n
  VI.5–6: i. 36n
Pacuvius, Marcus
Hermiona: fragment 177: vi. 18n
Paul, The Apostle
Ad Hebraeos (Epistle to the Hebrews): 11:1: iv. 2n
Paulus Iulius
Digesta: Pro Socio (Digest: For a Partner): XVII.2.3.2: iii. 40n, 42n
Digesta: De Operibus Libertorum (Digest: On the Right of Freeman): XXXVIII1.16: iv. 9n
Persius, A. Flaccus
Satura (Satires):

I.351c–d: iii. 11n
VII.521c–d: vi. 27n
VII.522b–c: vi. 27n
VII.526a–c: vi. 27n
Plato (Pseudo-)
  Axiochus: 365e: i. 29n, vi. 12n
Plautus, Titus Maccius
  Aulularia (The Pot of Gold): 724–25: ii. 32n
  Bacchides (The Two Bacchises): 1057: iii. 17n
  Cistellaria (The Casket): 211–12: ii. 34n
  Poenulus (The Little Carthaginian): 312: vi. 2n
Pliny, Gaius Caecilius Secundus (Pliny the Younger)
  Panegyrics: 36.3: ii. 39n
Pliny, Gaius Secundus (Elder)
  Natural History:
    II.5, 14: i. 29n
    XXIX.1, 2: i. 27n
    XXXVII.2, 7: i. 30n
Plotinus
  Enneada (Enneads):
    V.1.2: i. 13n
    VI.4.12: i. 13n
Plutarch
  Alexander: 8.2: v. 22n
  Caesar: 11.5–6: v. 23n
  Cato m.: 21.7–8: iii. 14n
  Cicero synk.: 5: iii. 14n
  Institutiones Lacedaemoniorum (The Ancient Customs of the Spartans): 25: v. 12n
  Lycurgus:
    13.1–4: v. 9n
    17.6: v. 11n
    18.2: v. 11n
Politian (Poliziano, Angiolo Ambrogini)
  Nuncia: lines 182–187: i. 36n
Psalms (Bible) 82 (Vulgate 81): 6: i. 28n
Quintilian, Marcus Fabius
  Institutio Oratoria (Rules of Rhetoric and Education):
    I.4.22: vi. 31n
    I.5.56: iii. 43n
    I.10.1: i. 3n
    I.10.46–49: v. 19n

VIII.1.3: iii. 43n
X.1.32: iii. 23n
X.1.109: iii. 21n
Sallust, Gaius Crispus
  Bellum Catilinae (The War with Catiline):
    2.8: ii. 4n
    5.8: iv. 16n
    12.2: iv. 16n
    13.3: iii. 7n
    61.4: ii. 13n
  Bellum Jugurthinum (The War with Jugurtha):
    1.3–4: iii. 44n
    2.3: i. 14n
    63.6: vi. 10n
    89.7: iii. 7n
Scaliger, Iulius Caesar
  Poetices Libri (Poetry Books): V: iii. 44n
Seneca, Lucius Annaeus
  Ad Lucilium. Epistulae Morales (Epistles: To Lucilius):
    4.1: v. 17n
    4.2: ii. 25n
    13.8: ii. 23n
    13.16: ii. 35n
    15.9: ii. 33n
    23.9–10: ii. 35n
    24.13: ii. 24n
    44.7: ii. 45n
    48.11: ii. 43n
    59.14: ii. 43n
    60.4: ii. 4n
    73.12–13: ii. 43n
    76.23: ii. 48n
    76.35: ii. 51n
    78.10: ii. 46n
    85.8: iii. 2n
    87.19: ii. 43n
    90.28: ii. 37n
    92.30: ii. 43n
    101.4: ii. 35n
    102.21: ii. 37n
    120.2–3: iv. 13n
    124.3: ii. 47n

De Brevitate Vitae (On the Shortness of Life): 1–2: v. 3n
De Otio (On Leisure: to Serenus): 4.1: ii. 38n, v. 17n
Seneca, Marcus Annaeus
  Controversiae (Controversial Topics)
    II.10.4: iii. 15n
    IV.28.5: iii. 15n
Sextus Empiricus
  Adversum Mathematicos (Against the Mathematicians): I.3: iv. 8n
Suetonius, Gaius Tranquillus
  De Viris Illustribus (The Life of Illustrious Men):
    Caligula: 34.2: iii. 15n
    De Grammaticis (On Grammarians): 10: iii. 15n
Tacitus, Cornelius
  Agricola: 15.4: iv. 16n
  Annales (Annals): I.17: v. 5n
  Dialogus De Oratoribus (Dialogue on the Orators): 30.5: iii. 21n
Terence, Publius Afer
  Adelphi (The Brothers): 946: iii. 34n
  Andria (The Lady of Andros):
    86: iii. 48n
    126: vi. 3n
    171: iii. 49n
    214: vi. 10n
    378: vi. 4n
    399: iii. 35n
    423: iii. 36n
    639: vi. 9n
  Eunuchus (The Eunuch):
    42: iii. 26n
    134: ii. 6n, iv. 5n
    186: iii. 34n
    252: iii. 39n
    908: iii. 49n
  Heauton Timorumenos (The Self-Tormentor):
    77: vi. 14n
    84–85: vi. 15n
    86: vi. 16n
    218–220: iii. 26n
    360: iii. 34n
    574: ii. 15n
    688: iii. 37n
  Phormio:

List of Sources

44: ii. 32n
454: vi. 8n
Ulpian, Domitius
  Digesta: De Dolo Malo: (Digest: On Bad Faith) IV.3.1: iii. 41n
  Digesta: De Iure Patronatus (Digest: On the Right of the Advocate):
  XXXVII.14.1: iv. 9n
  Digesta: Pro Socio (Digest: For a Partner)
    XVII.2.29.2: iii. 19n
    XVII.52.4.56: iii. 19n
Varro, Marcus Terentius
  De Lingua Latina (On the Latin Language): VI.61.95: iv. 1n
Virgil, Publius Maro
  Aeneis (Aeneid):
    I.287: v. 26n
    II.304–8: iii. 22n
    IV.298: ii. 31n
    IV.617–18: ii. 21n
    V.231: i. 33n
    VI.278–79: ii. 18n
Vitruvius, Pollio
  De Architectura (On Architecture): I.8.12: i. 3n
Xenophon
  Memorabilia (Memorable Things): II.6.39: iii. 53n

General Index

❦

Achilles, 20, 121
Accursius, Franciscus, 79, 81
acuity:
  of mind (*mentis acies*), 40
  more acutely (*argutius*), 139
  wittily and truly (*argute et vere*),
    101
Adam, 74, 127
Alcesimarchus, 66
Alexander the Great, 20, 120–21
Amphion, 130–31
Anselm, 15
Apollo, 38, 48; temple of, 4
Aquadia, Felice, 22
Aquilius, Gaius Gallus, 85
Arab(s):
  skilled in letters, 116
  warfare, 121
Archimedes, 64
Aristotle, 1, 19, 80
  epithets against, 78
  metaphor valued by, 44, 130–31
arts and sciences (*bonae artes scientiaeque*), 98, 104
  fine arts, 122
  histories of, 133, 135
  liberal, 35–37, 49–50, 92–93, 100
  orb of, 129
  professors of, 77
  pursuit of, 52
  study of, 35, 92, 117, 125, 135

whole sphere of, 132
whole world of, 51
Asinius, Pollio, 77
Assyrians, 122
Athena, Pallas. *See* Minerva
Athens, Athenians, 82, 115, 119
Attica, 85
Attila, 113
Augustine, Saint, 5
Augustus, 122

Bacchus, 44
Bias, 38
Bible. See sacred books
Brant, Sebastian, 15–16

Caesar, Gaius Julius, 20, 120–21
  dialect in, 85
Caligula, 77
Campania, 116
Cannae, 115
Carafa, Antonio, 20
Carthage, Carthaginians, 64, 115–16
Cassirer, Ernst, 10
Cato, Marcus Publius (the Younger),
    77
Chaldeans, 122
Charles II (1661–1700), 52
Chilon of Sparta, 38
Chinese, 120
Chremes, 129

General Index

Cicero, Marcus Tullius, 4, 5, 7, 21,
24, 38–39, 77
eloquence of, 80, 86, 117
Circean potion, 75
Cleomenes of Sparta, 115
common consent, 117
common good:
of citizens, 95, 99
of greatest service to the greatest
number, 101
of letters, 105
commonwealth(s), 8, 35, 52, 57, 67,
104
Christian, 133
fight for, 111
fortunate, 132
legitimate, 117
principles of, 119
constellations:
Argus, 48
Dolphin, 130–31
Lyre, 48, 130–31
Ursa Minor, 137
Crassus, Marcus L., 63
Cujas, Jacques, 79
Cusanus, Nicolaus, 16–17
Cyrus, 122

Dante Alighieri, 103
Dark Ages, 121
Delphi, 2, 3, 4, 38
Democritus, 78, 80
Demosthenes, 47
and Cicero, 77, 86
Descartes, René, 89
Cartesian education, 2–3, 9, 14, 27
Cartesian method, 11, 23–26
and first philosophy, 81
pineal gland, 84
poetaster, 78
dialects:
Gallic, 85
in Livy, 85
Patavian, 85
Digest, Roman, 12
dynamics, 89

Egypt, 87
eloquence (eloquentia), 7, 21, 36, 48,
104, 118, 129–31, 138
Epictetus, 75

Epicurus, 22, 78, 97
Erasmus, Desiderius, 15–16
esoteric and exoteric, 22–23, 134–35,
139
Eurotas, 114

fables, 130–31
Fetiales, 71
first parent, 89
First Truth, 50, 93
Fisch, Max, 6, 24
folly (stultitia), 15, 58–59
fool(s) (stultus), 11, 15–16, 57–58,
65, 137
and happiness, 68
impetuousness, 130
joys of, 64
lack of wisdom, 63
weapon of, 61–62
fortune (fortuna and casus):
adverse, 62
dictates of, 114
dominion of, 110
hands of, 64, 70
Furies, 65

Galen, Claudius, 24, 81, 88n
geometry:
analytic, 22
awareness of, 50
demonstrations, 89
Euclidean, 22
figures, 132
forms, 64
method(s), 9, 81, 88, 118
proof, 50
See also Descartes, René; science(s)
God, 33, 39, 40, 58, 67, 93, 132–33,
134, 138
Almighty, (Deus Optimus Maxi-
mus), 40, 42, 66, 73, 96, 101,
137
continuous activity of, 41
divine Providence, 14, 56
divine wisdom, 8, 67
existence of, 45–46
omnipotent hand of, 57
Supreme Good, 80, 137
Supreme Will (summum Numen),
127–28
true divinity of, 96

General Index

military arts (*de re militari, bellica
ars,* and *artes belli*), 108, 111–
14, 117
power of, 121
praise of, 120
See also science(s)
Minerva, 42, 119
motherland (*patria*), 96–98
homeland, 61–62, 112
myth, 119

Naples:
city, 83
as state, 97
University of, 5–6, 12, 19
nations (*nationes, gentes*):
divine law of, 113
divine right of (*fas nationum*), 19, 117
major and minor, 42–43
mutual rights of people (*jus gen-
tium*), 118
powerful in war, 109
world of, 14
Nestor, 5
Nicolini, Fausto, 24, 143n
Nimrod, 127
Ninus, 122
Novaya Zemlya, 43

Olympus, Mount, 69
opinion(s), 56, 58, 70, 119, 137
clutter of, 127
deeply engraved, 136
false, 99
good, 103
to each his own, 128
oratory, 80, 137
Orpheus, 48, 130–31
ostentation, 36, 51, 76, 104
Ovid, Publius Naso, 24, 77, 80
Oziosi, Academy of, 13, 26

paideia, 14, 16, 18, 23, 37n
Palestine, 85
parent(s), 60, 104
advice of, 98
first, 89
pressure of, 126
passion(s), 16, 58
description of, 60–64
flux of, 128

freedom from, 80
for knowledge, 37
men subservient to, 55
perverse, 70
study prevented by, 51
unrestrained, 61
Peloponnesian War, 115
Persius, 65
Petrarch, 5, 17, 86n, 108n
Phaedrus, 16
phantasy (*phantasia*), 42–43, 47, 93
help of, 50
in youth, 136
Philo Judaeus, 16, 62, 65
philosopher(s), 4–5, 46, 77, 87–89,
111, 113, 121
most brilliant, 122
philosophy (*philosophia*):
dialectic, 118
divine, 45
first, 81
moral, 9–10, 33, 80, 118
nature of, 4–5
studies of, 79
See also metaphysics
physics, 24, 81, 133, 136
physical phenomena, 134, 137
Plato, 24, 27, 50, 70, 78, 88n
called divine, 80
sweetness of, 85
Plautus, 24, 66, 77, 80
poetry, 16, 25–26, 133, 134
poetic fables, 130
poetics, 80
poets, 50, 119
prudence (*prudentia*), 3, 6–12, 21–22
and fortitude, 20, 110
in human affairs, 138
See also wisdom
Ptolemy Philadelphus, 87
Pythagoras, 4–5, 38

Quintilian, Fabius, 139

reason (*ratio*), 40, 44, 55, 65, 136
age of, 45
divine, 67, 135
inquisitive, 93
as mind's eye (*oculus mentis*), 93
right, 74
as uniting men, 77

169

Library of Congress Cataloging-in-Publication Data

Vico, Giambattista, 1668–1744.
[Orazioni inaugurali, I–VI.   English]
  On humanistic education : (six inaugural orations, 1699–1707) /
Giambattista Vico ; from the definitive Latin text, introduction,
and notes of Gian Galeazzo Visconti ; translated by Giorgio A.
Pinton and Arthur W. Shippee ; with an introduction by Donald
Phillip Verene.
    p.   cm.
  Includes bibliographical references and index.
  ISBN 0-8014-2838-6 (cloth). — ISBN 0-8014-8087-6 (paper)
    1. Philosophy—Early works to 1800.   2. Theology—Early works to
1800.   3. Education, Humanistic—Early works to 1800.   I. Visconti,
Gian Galeazzo.   II. Title.
B3581.0742E5   1993
370.11′2—dc20   92-56787